MW00443420

An Executive Guide

CCPA

The Why, When, Where, What, and Who Guide to the

California Consumer Privacy Act -2018

~ 3 ~

Chapter 1 – The motivation behind the CCPA?

The popular telling of the tale goes that Alastair Mactaggart, a wealthy real estate developer in the Bay Area, became the most improbable, and perhaps the most audacious privacy activist in America through a causal conversation with a Google engineer at a dinner party. How this episode of political awakening came around was something more suited to a TV drama rather than the mundane real-world of legislative process even by Sacramento's flamboyant standard.

The story begins a few years ago, on a night in the hills above Oakland, Calif. where Alastair Mactaggart and his wife were entertaining some friends invited over for dinner. Coincidently, one of the guests was a software engineer at Google, the Internet Behemoth whose search and video sites are visited by over a billion people a month. As the evening settled in, Alastair Mactaggart asked his friend in casual conversation if he should be worried about the amount of information that Google collected about him. To Alastair Mactaggart's surprise his friend told him that if people realised how much Google really knows about them, they would flip out.

Now the enormity of this is that Alastair Mactaggart is no unworldly academic or swivel-eyed loon, he is a wealthy and successful businessman. Also, he had built his company on the back of condominiums in the Bay Area that provide the accommodation for the wealthy employees of Silicon Valley.

Nonetheless, he was taken aback by the reply, as he had never really thought about how companies like Google or Facebook monetized their businesses. He knew of course about the the vast pools of data they collected and monetized through directed marketing but these were abstractions, something he knew existed but had not given much thought or dwelled upon.

However, it was that casual social interaction that was the genesis for the improbable transformation of Alastair Mactaggart, from a successful property developer, a businessman, to an indefatigable privacy activist. Indeed over the next two years he and his team would be the bane of the Chamber of Commerce and the tech industry.

Suitably intrigued Mactaggart began to delve deeper into the business models and practices of the tech companies. He spent a lot of time researching their business models, taking a special interest in studying their opaque privacy policies. As a result, he duly learned about how tech businesses used online tracking and data trading to build profiles of users that could be traded through a data supply chain. And that there was no real limit on the information companies could collect or buy about him. To him this was frightening.

Furthermore, he discovered that in the United States there was no single, comprehensive law regulating the collection and use of personal data. There were rules and protocols but these were largely established by the very companies that harvested and traded in data. What is more, the consumers whose data was being harvested were unaware of the scale or the purpose of collection let alone the intrusiveness of the operation as details were obscured within privacy policies and end-user agreements most people never actually read.

As Alastair Mactaggart began to scrutinize these privacy policies closely, he discovered that buried in the legalese were clauses that effectively gave the business the user's consent for the collection, processing and sharing of a vast array of personal information. He soon was appalled at the duplicity of the respected tech giants and their methods employed for the misappropriation of personal information that was being collected and shared by online businesses. This was the catalysts that spurred his interest in online privacy and this led to a two-year effort, which he personally funded, to get a privacy law for California on the books.

Alastair Mactaggart was able to become a champion of consumer privacy simply because in California it is not just politicians and legislators that can propose new laws, residents can also propose new bills through a ballot initiative so long as they can show popular support by obtaining sufficient verifiable signatures. Ultimately, Alastair Mactaggart obtained more than double the amount of sufficient signatures to put a ballot initiative before the California voters in November 2018 that, if approved, would have enacted a data privacy law.

Initially, the signature collection effort for consumer privacy was a slow process. Volunteer activists had to canvas for support to gain signatories – going door-to-door or working the commuter trains - from Californians that despite working for tech companies would still hopefully support such a privacy bill. Perhaps, it was this lack of traction that may have initially flat-footed the tech industry for they appear to have been rather slow in their response to the ballot initiative.

However, the ballot initiative suddenly gained steam in the spring of 2018. Suddenly there was public support and whereas before there was apathy now there was energy. This was a process perhaps spurred by growing privacy concerns among the public, as a result of the Facebook data breach debacle in spring 2018. However, the Chamber of Commerce and the tech industry did awaken to the threat as they became concerned that the ballot initiative was gaining too much public support. Then they were quick to launch a campaign of opposition to try to derail and debunk the ballot initiative. Indeed, later, when the state legislature and the tech companies realised that the ballot initiative had overwhelmingly public support that exceeded the required number of verified signatories they became alarmed to the far-reaching nature of the law. Importantly they were concerned with the fact that a ballot-driven law is more difficult to amend in the future, as to change or repeal it required a 70% vote in both houses and more likely a fresh ballot initiative.

Consequently, the legislature cut a deal with Alastair Mactaggart, to pass a somewhat watered down version of his bill in exchange for him withdrawing from the ballot due in November 2018. Thus the CCPA was abruptly negotiated, drafted, and shortly thereafter signed into law on June 28, 2018. It will go into effect on January 1, 2020. As it stands the CCPA is arguably the most significant advance in privacy protection introduced in the United States.

The surge in public support

One suggestion for the late surge in popular support for Alastair Mactaggart's ballot initiative is that in the spring of 2018 the EU's

General Data Protection Regulation (GDPR) came into effect and combined with the Cambridge Analytica scandal made consumer data privacy a hot topic. As a result Alastair Mactaggart's main question, which is, 'in a world where most people have no choice but to have a phone or computer, how can they maintain control over their personal data to ensure it, stays personal?' – chimed well with the sentiments of the time.

Indeed, his goal of developing a privacy law focusing on transparency, control and accountability dovetailed well with public sentiment. The citizens of California were growing increasingly concerned and impatient with the seemingly never ending stream of breaches and the nonchalant attitude of the tech giants towards consumer privacy. Mactaggart's ballot initiative was a timely banner to gather beneath as it introduced three pillars for consumer privacy; transparency, control and accountability and that proved popular with potential voters. The 3 pillars became the basis of the ballot initiative created by Californians for Consumer Privacy: the California Consumer Rights Privacy Act, which surged forward in the late spring of 2018 catching their opponents for once off-guard.

The bill received 625,000 signatures, which is almost twice the number required for an initiative to be included on the California ballot.

The Catalyst for CCPA

During the spring of 2018 there was no escaping the deluge of stories about Cambridge Analytica and Facebook. The mainstream media interest peaked when a pink-haired ex-Cambridge Analytica academic regaled his story to The Guardian and The New York Times. Not to be outdone TV journalists at Channel 4 News secured undercover footage of Cambridge Analytica executives boasting of their successes using their controversial techniques and services. There was unsurprisingly a backlash against Cambridge Analytica and Facebook. Questions about the use and misuse of personal data therefore were high in the public's mind as Alastair Mactaggart's ballot initiative entered the final crucial few months of the 2-year campaign. If that was not bad enough for the tech industry, things could have been much worse as Google also had suffered an almost identical failure of process under it Google+ application, which has also compromised the personal information of over 50 million users. Google, fearful that a public scandal would accelerate and fuel the demand for privacy regulation on the tech industry fixed the vulnerability in 3 days and then decided to keep quiet. Google's shameful act of concealing the compromise of over 50 million users personal information would only surface in the fall of 2018. In the meantime Facebook took the full brunt of the public fury but not without some justification. This was because in addition to the Cambridge Analytica catastrophe they had further major breaches in July and a hugely damaging breach in September which compromised around 90 million accounts.

Public confidence in the tech industries ability to protect their personal information plummeted and their anxiety rocketed with the breaking news of yet another security blunder. Indeed in 2018 alone there were major breaches that occurred that were eminently preventable had security controls been in place. One such example pertinent to Californians was that in February, an anonymous attacker seized two databases owned and operated by

The Sacramento Bee, a daily newspaper published in Sacramento, California. One of those IT assets contained California voter registration data provided by California's Secretary of State, while the other stored contact information for subscribers to the newspaper. According to The Sacramento Bee, the hack exposed 53,000 subscribers' information along with the personal data of 19.4 million California voters.

Why Businesses should be concerned

Underpinning the Ballot campaign was the desire to protect consumer privacy through the creation of a set of rights roughly analogous to certain of the rights under the GDPR in Europe. Consequently, after a lot of the horse-trading between the legislators and Alastair Mactaggart's team, the CCPA will grant California residents the right to access, delete, port out, and opt out of the sale of their personal information. Currently, Personal information is very broadly defined and it includes anything that relates to a person, household or device. The law also requires certain disclosures about personal information collection and sharing practices, such as once enforced, businesses will have to inform consumers' of the purposes for collecting and selling their personal information and the subsequent identification of those to whom it is being sold. In addition there will be the right to opt-out of the sale or sharing of personal information and importantly, the business is not allowed to discriminate against those exercising their rights. For example, a business must not charge consumers that exercise their right to opt-out any fees to access their information or service or by offering them a different level of service or pricing.

As the CCPA law was drafted and passed so quickly using the controversial gutting-and-amending technique it has many nuances, contradictions, unclear provisions, and apparent unintended consequences. As a result many of these provisions may be subsequently changed or refined in 2019. For example, the broad definitions of a consumer and what constitutes personal information will be targeted for change by the tech industry. However, interestingly, although the ballot initiative and the subsequent CCPA came under concerted attack from many sectors of business and commerce its opponents made few tangible gains. For instance a conglomeration of businesses as diverse as banks, tech start-ups, automobile associations and marketing groups proposed a wish-list of changes that amounted to circa 20 pages during the first clean-up review (SP 1211) of the CCPA act, but few and even then only minor changes were taken on-board by the legislators. Nonetheless, many industry observers think that 2019 will see much more aggressive strategies by the tech companies and the chamber of commerce in trying to gut the bill. At present though, any for-profit business that is over $25 million in revenue or that handles California resident personal information on any material scale should immediately start to at least consider the necessity of compliance with the spirit of the privacy law. Fortunately for many, the introduction of GDPR in May 2018 means most businesses will have many of the technical and business controls in place for identifying, categorizing and protecting personal identifiable information that will need only to be adjusted in the context of the CCPA. However, for businesses that have chosen to ignore the EU GDPR for whatever reason they may well need to make substantial operational or business model changes to their company's practices and procedures.

Early attention to compliance is especially important given that the CCPA, in part, uses one of California's favoured approaches to consumer protection law enforcement by permitting a private right of action with statutory damages ($100-$750 per violation for private claims). Essentially, California residents will be able to sue businesses in the case of a data breach where they can show that the business did not have adequate protections for their person identifiable information. Under the CCPA, the plaintiff does not need to show actual harm to them although they must send a notice of their claims to the business and allow the business 30 days to cure. As is quite typical of the CCPA as it stands there is no indication as to how a business would cure a data breach. Nonetheless, there is provision for the California Attorney General (CaAG) to choose to take over or halt the private claim. Within the scope of the bill this provides a fairly limited path for private claims. However, in practice these claims will typically arise as class action lawsuits. In these real-world scenarios attorneys representing plaintiff classes will aggressively pursue businesses that have suffered a data breach fully confident that the business, facing significant litigation costs will settle the case long before reaching adjudication on the merits regardless of their fault in the breach. For instance, with statutory damages of $100 - $750 per violation for private claims then a breach involving significant numbers of individuals could result in a potential exposure of many tens or even hundreds of millions of dollars.

Why did this come about?

Throughout 2018 there have been many large breaches of person identifiable information from a host of large companies but none captured the public and media's attention more that the Facebook-Cambridge Analytica scandal. However, to a public with a high tolerance and a nonchalant indifference to the monotonous regularity of data breaches, why did the Cambridge Analytica scandal in particular rise above the ever present drone and toll so loudly.

Why Facebook –Cambridge Analytica was a scandal

The Facebook– Cambridge Analytica data wrong-doing was a major political scandal in early 2018. The breach of up to 85 million Facebook users personal information came to light when it was revealed that Cambridge Analytica, a company that had worked on Donald Trump's US presidential election campaign, had harvested the personal data of millions of people's Facebook profiles without their consent and used it for political purposes. The scandal has been described as a watershed moment in the public understanding of personal data privacy. It also resulted directly in a precipitous fall in Facebook's stock price and subsequent calls for tighter regulation of tech companies' use of data.

Facebook

Facebook is adamant that it was not a breach of their security or controls and from a strictly technical definition of a breach that may be true. However there is no doubt that up to 85m subscribers' data was released unintentionally. The failure came about as a result of Facebook's policy of sharing subscriber data with third parties under the pretext of research. To understand how this catastrophe unfolded we need to understand that part of Facebook's service is that external organisations and developers can build apps and other services that access data about Facebook users. For example, many subscribers actively play games with their friends on Facebook. In doing so, these subscribers are providing usage and performance metrics that are of interest to the game developers and helpful in improving their product by increasing user interaction within Facebook. However, the developers behind games and other apps also have access to data that Facebook holds about the subscribers including their friends. The scope of personal data can range from access to basic profile information through to text chat histories and all of the photos and videos they have uploaded.

The way the Facebook - Cambridge Analytica breach arose was that back in 2015, around 270,000 Facebook users were paid to use an app called 'thisisyourdigitallife' that connected to their Facebook accounts. The app was built by Global Science Research, which claimed it would use access to the data for research purposes. The app included a personality test that people could take to learn more about themselves. Users were required to give it permission to access data about them already held by Facebook, such as their likes, posts and other activity. But critically the app also gained access to data about all of the users' friends too, unless they had changed their default privacy settings. As a result,

~ 15 ~

the app surreptitiously collected data from more than 85 million Facebook users from a consent base of only 270k users.

This was possible due to a feature that meant apps could ask for permission to access in addition to the user's data all the data related to their Facebook friends. This was clearly meant for research only but Global Science Research is reported to have sold the data it had collected to Cambridge Analytica. In turn Cambridge Analytica is suspected of then combining the data with other sources in order to profile users for their own political ends. Consequently, Cambridge Analytica was able to boast to clients that it can 'find your voters and move them to action' through data-driven campaigns and a team that includes data scientists and behavioural psychologists.

Indeed Cambridge Analytica claimed on their website that they held data on more than 230 million American voters as well as boasting of their recent political campaign success. 'Within the United States alone, we have played a pivotal role in winning presidential races as well as congressional and state elections'.

The connection between Cambridge Analytica and Facebook only came to light In December 2016. This was when Carole Cadwalladr came across Cambridge Analytica while researching the US presidential election. The company's boastful manner and chequered track record interested her as it belied its bland, academic-sounding name. Indeed the impression they liked to project was that they were associated or closely affiliated with Cambridge University in the UK. However, the more Cadwalladr delved into the company the more secretive but intriguing they became. Gradually her persistence enabled her network of sources to grow to include former employees, academics, lawyers and others concerned about the tactics employed by Cambridge Analytica and associates and their detrimental effect on democracy.

Importantly her initial investigations uncovered the role of US billionaire Robert Mercer in the US election campaign: his strategic "war" on mainstream media and his political campaign funding, some apparently linked to Brexit – the UK's referendum to leave the EU.

The Facebook Algorithm

The way that Global Science Research's app was able to harvest data about consenting subscriber and their non-consenting Facebook friends was via a Facebook algorithm with very broad and poorly crafted permissions. However, Cambridge Analytica had their algorithm that trawled through the most obvious of indicators of preference; the "likes" users' will use to up-vote as they browse the site. As these likes are reliable indicators of preference they are high-value data points when gathering sensitive personal information about sexual orientation, race, gender, politics, even intelligence.

The importance to Cambridge Analytica was that just a few dozen "likes" per user can give a strong prediction of which party they will vote for and it can do all this without any need for delving into personal messages, posts, status updates, photos or all the other information Facebook holds. What's more people were not particularly bothered about their likes being publicly viewable. However, five years ago psychology researchers showed that far more complex traits could be deduced from patterns in profiles by algorithms that were invisible to a human observer. Just a few apparently random "likes" could form the basis for disturbingly complex character assessments.

Some of the consistent correlations noted in a paper in the Proceedings of the National Academy of Sciences journal in 2013 were surprising, such as when users liked "curly fries" and Sephora cosmetics, this was said to give clues to intelligence; Hello Kitty likes indicated political views; "Being confused after waking up from naps" was linked to sexuality.

However most worrying was that, "Few users were associated with 'likes' explicitly revealing their attributes. For example, less than 5% of users labelled as gay were connected with explicitly gay groups, such as No H8 Campaign," the peer-reviewed research found. The problem then was this inconvenient disparity between inferred (algorithm) and declared (Likes) personal characteristics.

At the time Facebook "likes" were public by default and the researchers, Michal Kosinski, David Stillwell and Thore Graepel, raised privacy concerns stating that;

"The predictability of individual attributes from digital records of behaviour may have considerable negative implications, because it can easily be applied to large numbers of people without their individual consent and without them noticing.

"Commercial companies, governmental institutions, or even your Facebook friends could use software to infer attributes such as intelligence, sexual orientation or political views that an individual may not have intended to share."

What is deemed a privacy concern for some may be deemed to be a business opportunity to others. By early 2014, Cambridge

Analytica chief executive Alexander Nix had signed a deal with one of Kosinski's Cambridge colleagues, lecturer Aleksandr Kogan, for a private commercial venture. Importantly the private venture was to be separate from Kogan's duties at Cambridge University, but was to be heavily influenced by Kosinski's work.

The result was a Facebook app which featured a personality quiz, and Cambridge Analytica paid for people to take it, advertising on platforms such as Amazon's Mechanical Turk.

The true purpose of the app was in addition to recording the results of each quiz, was also to collect data from the participants' Facebook account – as well as to extract the data of their Facebook friends. This was needed to seek out patterns and build an algorithm to predict results for other Facebook users. Their friends' profiles provided a testing ground for the formula. However to make the algorithm politically valuable the participants needed to have a Facebook account and be a US voter. This was so that tens of millions of the profiles could be matched to electoral rolls. Hence, from an initial trial of 1,000 "seeders", the researchers obtained 160,000 profiles – or about 160 per person. Eventually a few hundred thousand paid test-takers would be the key to data from a vast swath of US voters.

Despite its obvious attraction it was illicit, primarily because Kogan did not have permission to collect or use data for commercial purposes. His permission from Facebook to harvest profiles in large quantities was specifically restricted to academic use. Nonetheless, Facebook did at the time allow apps to collect friends' data, but it was only for use in the context of Facebook itself, to encourage interaction. Selling that data on, or putting it to other purposes, – including Cambridge Analytica's political marketing – was strictly forbidden. It is also likely the project was breaking EU data protection laws, which ban sale or use of personal data without consent and that includes cases where consent is given for one purpose but data is used for another. In this scenario the paid test-takers signed up to T&Cs, including collection of their own data, but Facebook's default terms allowed their friends' data to be collected as well, unless they had changed their privacy settings. But none of them agreed to their data possibly being used to create a political marketing tool or to it being placed in a vast campaign database. Despite this, Kogan maintains everything he did was legal and says he had a "close working relationship" with Facebook, which had granted him permission for his apps.

Not surprisingly, Facebook denies this was a data breach. Vice-president Paul Grewal said: "Protecting people's information is at the heart of everything we do, and we require the same from people who operate apps on Facebook. If these reports are true, it's a serious abuse of our rules."
Nonetheless, the scale of the data collection that Cambridge Analytica paid for whether illicit or not was so large that within months, Kogan and Cambridge Analytica had a database of millions of US voters. Furthermore they had their own algorithm to scan them, identifying likely political persuasions and personality traits. They could then decide who to target and craft their messages so they were likely to appeal to those individuals – this is a political approach known as "micro-targeting".

What made the Facebook Graph API's v1.0 highly problematic were its extended permissions. Apps could request a huge range of a users' friend's info without much friction or communicating the reason(s) for providing consent.

Once authorized with a single prompt, v1.0 app could potentially remain in the background collecting and processing people's data—and that of their entire friend network—for years. Additionally, v1.0 apps could also request users' private messages (i.e. their Facebook DM inbox) via the "read_mailbox" API request. The scale of the breach can be determined by the potential scope of the users' FRIENDS info that could be made available: About me, actions, activities, b-day, check-ins, education, events, games, groups, hometown, interests, likes, location, notes, online status, tags, photos, questions, relationships, religion/politics, status, subscriptions, website, and work history.

Fortunately, since the app was built, Facebook's API, privacy controls and terms of service have changed multiple times. Indeed, the present Facebook Graph API's v2.0 is far more restrictive by default. Facebook users have long complained that the service's privacy settings and data collection information was too complicated and hard to find. In an effort to reduce that confusion, the company has come out with a new privacy guide to go along with an updated data collection policy.

The changes come in prelude to new European Union rules that take effect on May 25 requiring companies to add more privacy controls and clearly disclose how and why they collect user data. The changes will eventually affect all Facebook users regardless of location, but they will first roll out in Europe.

Facebook, the world's largest social network, revamped the policies it uses when collecting data on the more than 2 billion people who use it every month. As part of the new policy, released April 19, the company is also spelling out more clearly how it collects and uses that information about you.

However, the new policy comes in at more than 4,200 words so brevity was not a major consideration. The verbose language is meant to be easy to understand, but did they really expect anyone to read this before they sign up? However, perhaps an unintentional consequence of this verbose document is that it helps a motivated person better understand how the company turns consumer data into personalized recommendations, tailored advertisements and academic research.

While Facebook's new privacy and data collection policies are more clearly laid out, gone is much of the impenetrable legalese, it's still a lot of information for a casual user to possibly digest. However to spare the anguish here are the main takeaways from the new data policy.

- Facebook collects data about everything you share
- Specifically, Facebook collects all the content that its users provide from when they sign up, upload or share content, and notably, when they communicate with others on Facebook. But it's not strictly under the user's control for if others should post a photo of the user, post something about that user, upload or sync their contact info or message them — then Facebook collects that information as well.

- Facebook users have a number of ways to spend money through the service including in-game purchases and donations. Whenever you pay for something through the site, Facebook collects information about the transaction, including payment information like debit and credit card numbers, authentication information, and billing and shipping details.
- Facebook shares some information with researchers and developers but does not sell personal information on individuals to advertisers or take any part in trading data within the data supply chain ecosystem. Facebook founder and CEO Mark Zuckerberg testified before Congress that Facebook does not sell individuals personal information instead Facebook uses that information internally to target ads.
- The new data policy reveals how Facebook handles ads and user data. The company says it only shares non-personally identifiable information like telling an advertiser that an ad did well with a certain demographic. In addition to advertisers, Facebook also provides some information to service providers or vendors that provide technical support, customer support or other services.
- Facebook is making some privacy changes including prompting users about whether they want to keep sharing political or religious information and whether they want to allow targeted ads. Users already have the ability to turn off targeted ads and remove religious or political information from their profiles, but now users will specifically be asked about those matters.

- Users in the EU and Canada must now opt into allowing Facebook to use facial recognition technology to suggest friends to tag in photos and videos or to detect when others may be trying to use your image as their profile picture. Users previously had to choose to turn the feature off rather than opt in.
- Facebook already has certain safety settings for users ages 13 to 18, but now they will also need a parent or guardian's permission to allow some features like seeing targeted ads in certain countries (Facebook doesn't say who it will get parental consent or how it will verify that any consent is legitimate). However, Facebook will continue to collect information about minor's use of the site, regardless of their ad targeting preference. And regardless of location, Facebook will prompt those users globally on whether they want targeted ads or not.

The changes to the Privacy Policy come at a time when people are closely watching how Facebook reacts to the intense scrutiny into their data privacy processes. So concerned where congress that the US lawmakers summoned Facebook CEO Mark Zuckerberg to Washington for two days of questioning about why Facebook failed to adequately safeguard as many as 87 million users' privacy.

The user is the product

The updated policy includes one of Facebook's most frequently repeated refrains: "We don't sell any of your information to anyone, and we never will." So how did it come to ring up more than $40 billion in revenue in 2017? In large part, it does this by selling access to not just the vast Facebook user-base but to high-specific and well matched individual users based on their characteristic profile.

"We use the information we have about you -- including information about your interests, actions and connections -- to select and personalize ads, offers and other sponsored content that we offer you," the policy says.

In the Facebook business model they are effectively the middle man matching and connecting advertisers to the user. This direct marketing is effective due to the precise level of detail Facebook has collected or produced - inferred through algorithms - about their users' characteristics, location and personal connections. Nonetheless, it is still overwhelming for most casual users to learn just how much info Facebook has on them. In a similar way to how the Google engineer responded so candidly to Mactaggart's query of whether he should be concerned, then yes there is reason for concern. For instance, Facebook has a listing for what it thinks each user's political views are. It infers this information from a mixture of photos, videos and thoughts posted on the user's timeline. It also gleans data and further inferences from their interactions with Facebook friends, as well as the pages and posts they "like."

Moreover, the company is not content with information about the user it wants to know everything so it collects seven different kinds of information from the devices they use. That includes data about the version of software you're running, how low your battery is and how much storage you have left on your device. On top of that, Facebook can access information about devices that are connected to the same network you're on.

This kind of info is often used for something industry experts call fingerprinting, which is how websites identify a user based on all the data they can collect from the device. Tying that fingerprint to a Facebook account is a very powerful tool for tracking, allowing companies and advertisers to more easily identify you across the internet – even when you are not on Facebook.

However this tracking isn't always nefarious as it is often has a legitimate purpose such as enabling some Facebook services to work easily by configuring the service to match the device capabilities such as when streaming video from a device to a TV.

What are my Facebook friends telling app creators about me?

One alarming element of the Cambridge Analytica scandal was how a relatively small group of Facebook users -- about 270,000 of them -- were able to share information on so many millions of users. It happened because Facebook allows apps to collect data on a user's entire network of Facebook friends, and only the user interacting with the app has to give consent.

In 2015, Facebook limited the kinds of data third-party apps can collect on its users, years before news about Cambridge Analytica broke. In the new policy posted to its website, Facebook tells users it's trying to limit this access even further. "For example, we will remove developers' access to your Facebook and Instagram data if you haven't used their app in three months," the policy says.

But some collection of data through friends' apps will continue. To totally shut this down, a user will have to give up using any apps at all through their Facebook account.

How long does Facebook keep my data?

That depends. If you delete -- not deactivate, actually delete -- your account, Facebook will delete your posts, including photos and status updates. But that doesn't include the data Facebook got about you from sources other than yourself. So everything Facebook learned about you from your friends, from data brokers and from other websites, is kept for as long as the social network wants it.

The company also hangs onto information it might need for legal reasons, and to prevent abuse on its platform. "For example, if relevant, we exchange with third-party partners about the reliability of your account to prevent fraud, abuse and other harmful activity on and off our products," the policy says.

Do I have any say in this?

You can adjust your settings to change how much of your profile is public and how much you share with third-party apps, as well as other settings. But when it comes to the data policy, you don't have much of a choice. You have to take it or leave it.

In this case, "leave it" means leaving Facebook.

However, fresh from a grilling in the US Senate, Facebook has also been issued with a stern warning from the European Union regarding its data privacy policy. The EU Commissioner in charge of consumer rights, Věra Jourová, has told the social media platform that its terms and agreements are 'misleading' and despite two years of back and forth, users are still no clearer about just how Facebook are using their personal data. Jourová added that if nothing changes between now and December 31st, Facebook will face sanctions from national authorities. While Facebook is not the only tech company to face criticism from the EU over its data policies, it's under more scrutiny than most due to its links to Cambridge Analytica and the role it played in the UK's EU referendum two years ago.

However, for most users, Facebook's data collection and opting in user to certain data collection practices will not change. Instead, users will, in some cases, be more directly asked, and information about what data is being collected will be more clearly disclosed. Facebook itself said it is not asking for new rights "to collect, use or share your data on Facebook" or changing any of users' previous privacy choices.

The social media giant's appetite for your personal data combined with its ability to exploit it for profit regardless of societal cost has soured many on the company. But as we collectively reckon with the havoc Facebook has wrought, it's important to take stock of the other 800-pound gorillas in the digital room: Google and Amazon.

Amazon

Amazon has the world's largest online retail store has collected vast amounts of data on the people that use its services, and, like Facebook, shows so-called "interest based ads" to people targeted by the algorithms powered through this information. Essentially, these are targeted ads that take advantage of the information Amazon has collected on a customer to predict the future purchase of products that Amazon thinks they have a high-probability to buy.

And Amazon's algorithms have a trove of personal data to work upon when performing these predictive analytical functions. According to the Amazon Privacy Notice, the company collects the following data on those who visit Amazon.com:

- Amazon collects any information you enter on the Amazon Web site or give them in any other way
- Customer details such as name, address , phone numbers, post code
- credit card information
- The people to whom purchases have been shipped, including addresses and phone number
- The people (with addresses and phone numbers) listed in 1-Click settings
- The e-mail addresses of friends and other people
- The content of reviews and e-mails to us
- personal description and photograph in 'Your Profile'
- financial information, including Social Security and driver's license numbers
- The Internet protocol (IP) address used to connect your computer to the Internet

- Data on login credentials, email addresses and any Amazon passwords
- Data about the visitors computer or devices and any connection information such as browser type, version, and time zone setting, browser plug-in types and versions, operating system, and OS platform
- Data regards "purchase history, which Amazon sometimes aggregate with similar information from other customers to create features like Top Sellers"
- Tracking the "the full Uniform Resource Locator (URL) clickstream such as which web site the user came from, which pages they visited, and which website they departed for from Amazon's Web site, including date and time"
- The products the visitor viewed or searched for
- The phone number the visitor used to call the 800 number
- The session information, including page response times, download errors, length of visits to certain pages, page interaction information (such as scrolling, clicks, and mouse-overs), and methods used to browse away from the page
- Any information about the visitors location and their mobile device, including a unique identifier for the device

But that's not all, of course as Amazon also scores data on you from other sources. Some examples of that include:
- credit history
- Voting register
- The search term and search result information from some searches conducted through the Web search features offered by the Amazon subsidiary, Alexa Internet

- The search results and links, including paid listings (such as Sponsored Links)

Amazon however is not just an online retailer as it now is a leader in the Cloud providing services based upon their Amazon Web Services (AWS) operation. However, as the cloud scales so do the threats to security and they increase at logarithmic scale. Amazon also has their Alexa Internet division but the potential for Alexa to create privacy issues is causing come concern. Alexa and Echo a sister product stores transcripts of voice interactions users have with the digital assistants in order to "improve the accuracy of the results provided to you and to improve our services". The problem though is that innovation and competition has forced the manufacturers of these personal assistants to push the envelope. The result is some highly dubious features for privacy such as the addition of a camera designed to take regular pictures in order to help you get fashion advice. While its intended use might be innovative, from a privacy perspective the random taking snap - shots of the Echo's surroundings and storing them on Amazon's servers is fraught with issues. But astonishingly that is not the worst privacy killer for the echo also has a screen and camera which enables video conferencing and somewhere a developer thought it a good idea to enable Drop-in. The Drop-in feature is a way to allow you to video call a trusted friend without them confirming the call. Normally, when you initiate a call, the other party must accept. But if you enable Drop-In for a certain user, calling them will allow you to start seeing video from their Echo. Finally, Amazon records all the voice interactions with Alexa as transcripts against the customer's profile but it also introduces a unique form of direct marketing which is not nearly so easily detected by the user as the vocal responses have no obvious indicators that the response was from a sponsored advertisement.

However, Despite Amazon's vast trove of consumer data it is probably true that Amazon likely knows significantly less on the average American than Google or Facebook. And while Amazon insists that it is "not in the business of selling [Information about our customers] to others," that doesn't mean the company isn't sharing it with others. As you recall, Facebook didn't sell any personal data to Cambridge Analytica, either. Rather, it allowed a researcher to use an app to gather that data which then made its way into the hands of the analytics company.

Amazon, of course, does share some customer data with third parties. The company's privacy page provides a few examples of companies that may end up with some of your Amazon data via their joint offerings: "Starbucks, OfficeMax, Verizon Wireless, Sprint, T-Mobile, AT&T, J&R Electronics, Eddie Bauer and Northern Tool + Equipment."
Specifically, insists Amazon, the data shared is limited to "information related to those transactions."

Amazon through its retail website, Echo, Prime memberships, and myriad of other products and services is able to amass huge amounts of information on its customers and users. However, all that pales in comparison to Google.

Google

Google's catalogue of services and products is so vast — Search, Gmail, Google Maps, Drive, YouTube, AdWords, Chrome, Android, and Nest, just to name a few — that the data it gathers is likewise all encompassing.

Within Google's Privacy Policy they detail what categories and type of data they collect:

- Data on web searches;
- Websites visited;
- Videos watched;
- Ads clicked on or tapped;
- Geolocation;
- Device information;
- IP address and cookie data;
- Emails sent and received on Gmail;
- Contacts;
- Calendar events;
- Photos and videos uploaded;
- Docs, Sheets, and Slides on Drive
- Name
- Email address and password
- Birthday
- Gender
- Phone number
- Country

Now that might at first glance look relatively modest but from that list there is a high probability if you use a mobile device that Google knows most places and at what time you've visited. What's more they know what you search for day in and day out, and your entire digital network of friends and family. And this goes back to the time you started using their services.

Notably, like Facebook, Google insists that it doesn't sell your data. "We use data to show you these ads," the company explains, "but we do not sell personal information like your name, email address, and payment information."

And of course it doesn't, as that would run directly contrary to its business model of using the information it has on you as a selling point to advertisers. Google like Facebook and Amazon have a voracious appetite for data, but it is in their interest to guard it jealously.

But privacy issues still arise such as the recent revelation and subsequent acknowledgement from Google regards a privacy issue concerning 3rd-Party access to consumers Gmail accounts. Gmail, which has over 1.4 billion users globally, lets third-party developers integrate services into its email platform, such as trip planners and custom relationship management systems.

"Developers may share data with third parties so long as they are transparent with the users about how they are using the data," Susan Molinari, VP of public policy and government affairs for the Americas at Google, said in the letter to Senators, which was obtained by CNNMoney.

Google also makes "the privacy policy easily accessible to users to review before deciding whether to grant access," she said. Users can view or remove app access on their Google Account page -- or they can choose to not download the app.

While Google itself has stopped scanning Gmail users' email, some third-party developers have created apps that can access consumers' accounts and scan their messages for marketing purposes, according to a new report in The Wall Street Journal. In some cases, it's not just the developers' computers but their human employees who are reading Gmail users' messages. Nonetheless, Google has long allowed software developers the ability to access users' accounts as long as users gave them permission. That ability was designed to allow developers to create apps that consumers could use to add events to their Google Calendars or to send messages from their Gmail accounts. But marketing companies have created apps that take advantage of that access to get insights into consumers' behaviour. The apps offer things such as price-comparison services or travel-itinerary planning, but the language in their service agreements allows them to view users' email as well. In fact, it's become a "common practice" for marketing companies to scan consumers' email.

It isn't clear how carefully Google is monitoring such uses. Many consumers may not be aware that they've given apps such access to their accounts. Even if they are, Facebook's Cambridge Analytica scandal offers a worrisome example of how similar access to consumer data can be abused.

Indeed Google did have its own day of privacy reckoning when it was forced to come clean on a breach, which exposed the details of 500,000 users of its Google+ social media platform. Google's poorly advised attempts at a cover-up was meant to quell any potential calls for regulation over digital privacy. What it did expose was the weasel words that tech giants use to explain away embarrassing lapses in security controls and processes. Google brazenly claimed this incident represented an "exposure" rather than a "breach" of data. What this means to me and you is that the personal data of 500,000 users was exposed for any bad guy to take, but Google had no hard evidence anyone did. Google's argument that it wasn't obliged to disclose the Google+ incident because it had fulfilled its legal obligations is almost certainly accurate but not ethical. Perhaps Google genuinely though that they could hide behind the distinction between exposure and breach but today the difference is miniscule when it comes to a company's reputation for managing and securing their consumers' personal data. In trying to avoid enflaming the privacy debate Google's decision proved damaging as the backlash from the media proves the days of the tech firms routinely sweeping exposures or privacy breaches under the carpet are fading fast. Indeed, despite the Google+ incident not appearing particularly egregious it does raise the question as to why Google felt so threatened by increased pressure for regulatory controls. It appears the tech giants are finally realising that transparency is now demanded and the bar for disclosure has changed because of pressure from the public and government to address consumer privacy diligently and not just perform lip service.

Who does the CCPA effect?

The problem that arises when the privacy policies of the major Internet Scale companies are examined is that all three of the largest are adamant that they do not sell their users data. Indeed when we consider their business models it would appear to be contradictory to their objectives with regards targeted advertising. So if it is not the Internet Behemoths such as Facebook, Google and Amazon that are the primary targets of the California Consumer Privacy Act – 2018, then who are? To answer that question perhaps we should look past the main collectors, hoarders and consumers of personal data and treat the problem through the lens of a product supply chain – a data supply chain.

The Data Supply Chain

In today's digital environment we are living in a data-driven society, consisting of global markets and economies, connected through ubiquitous access and data transfer to everything from everywhere and any time. In today's environment, data is everywhere: It's stored all around us, flowing not only within our organizations, but between companies and their business partners and vendors, and between consumers and their devices. It is these flows and tributaries that make up the sprawling network of interconnection throughout the global market that constitutes the data supply chain.

But so ubiquitous are the data flows it has become much more difficult to control the flow into and outside of the business. Data governance and regulatory compliance is no longer simply a discipline confined to large enterprises and organisations. Indeed data governance , risk and compliance (GRC) is now an essential discipline for all companies that collect, store process or share consumer personal data. Thus companies have a responsibility to limit the data they share with their outside partners but they must also ensure that their vendors and suppliers safeguard that data and use it only for its intended purpose and keep it valid and up to date.

Typically with e-commerce, online firms regularly gather and store consumers' information, browsing habits, clickstream data, and purchasing history. Online consumer data might be passed from one firm to the next within an information supply chain, comparable to a traditional supply chain in the offline world.

ithin this supply-chain narrative, consumers pass information to websites, which then pass the information to tracking companies. These in turn will collate the data into specific contexts before they too may also pass the data on to larger data aggregators. The Data Aggregators act as distributors online by holding consolidated information of many users across many contexts. In this model the Data aggregators, which are invisible to the consumer, gather and store consumer data across many contexts, which link information from multiple online sources into a behavioural profile and may add off-line data as well. The consumers of this compilation of contextual data are the Advertising networks. These entities are similarly hidden from the users, providing a marketplace for advertisers to buy or sell information in order to target ads. The problem is that the consumer will typically only know about – and provide consent to - the website with which they are interacting. The downstream supply chain for their data is kept deliberately opaque to them.

Furthermore, while websites have long been known to record users' online activities in order to suggest products or give discounts, additional actors and technologies have entered the online tracking space with increasing access to user information. For example, a Web beacon can capture detailed information such as clicking, typing, and browsing behaviour and then relay that information to professional tracking companies and data aggregators. In addition, a mobile software company —with which no end customer has any direct contact—can log customer activity on mobile devices down to the keystroke for later analysis without the knowledge let alone the consent of the user. Primary websites may pass information to affiliated companies, sell information to data aggregators and data exchanges directly, or allow a tracking company to place an invisible beacon or web bug on their website whilst the consumer remains blissfully unaware that their personal data is being traded and perhaps profiled for uses they may never have agreed too.

These are the common strategic choices of firms collecting consumer data online within the current network of online tracking;

1) They can respect your data and privacy or

2) Find ways to undermine your privacy and rights then sell on your data.

This issue here is that the consumer has no agreement, contract or even in most cases even an awareness of the existence of these data aggregators and ad networks. An example of how vast these entities can be – that are hiding in plain sight – is to contemplate the recent breach of the Data Aggregator, Apollo back in the summer of 2018. Apollo claim on their website and its marketing materials to have 200 million contacts and information from over 10 million companies in its vast reservoir of data. And this was no sales and marketing exaggeration because a security practitioner from Night Lion Security, Vinny Troia, who routinely scans the internet for unprotected, freely accessible databases, discovered Apollo's trove containing 212 million contact listings as well as nine billion data points related to companies and organizations. All of which was readily available online, for anyone to access.

Apollo's core product it seems is data enrichment which is creating comprehensive profiles of individuals that can then be used for commercial purposes. Apollo achieved this by collecting and collating data from both publicly available information, but also data scraping websites, or trading through a web of business and employee connections. In addition to names, contact information, and job titles for employees, the data also includes things like the dates companies were founded, revenue numbers, keywords associated with the work companies do, number of employees, and website ranking by the Amazon-owned analytics company Alexa. The service then uses all of this information to try to draw connections between companies and identify possible sales opportunities.

A serious issue is that Apollo is certainly not the first large Data Aggregator to be breached who held enriched profiled information on people who have no idea their personal information has been used in this fashion. It is important to acknowledge though it is Apollo's customers that provided access to their own customers, but the fact remains that hundreds of millions of people out there have no idea who Apollo or these other Data Aggregators are let alone why their enriched profile information came to be exposed.

The importance of the CCPA is that it shifts the focus from the individuals making an informed choice, to justifying the roles and responsibilities of the firms gathering, aggregating, and using consumers' interests or behaviour online. Firms online are uniquely positioned to undercut or to respect privacy expectations. These firms benefit from aggregating and analysing consumer data and have an associated responsibility to not only minimize the harm to consumers but also to enact change where the firm is in the most knowledgeable and powerful position.

It is against this backdrop of data privacy carnage that Alastair Mactaggart enters the stage. He is a wealthy real estate businessman with no significant history in the fields of technology or consumer privacy. Alastair Mactaggart's main claim is that in a world where most people have no choice but to have a phone or computer, how can they maintain control over their personal data to ensure it stays personal? With this in mind he worked to develop a privacy initiative addressing these issues focusing on transparency, control and accountability. These three principles form the basis of the ballot initiative created by Californians for Consumer Privacy, the California Consumer Privacy Act (CCPA).

In California, the power to introduce legislation is not just limited to politicians. Under California law, citizens can propose new laws and constitutional amendments, and may secure a state wide vote on their initiatives if they get enough signatures on a petition advocating that the proposed law appear on a future ballot. The proponents of an initiative begin by circulating a petition, and once the requisite number of signatures is qualified by the Secretary of State, the initiative is approved to appear on the upcoming ballot. If approved by California voters, the initiative becomes state law – but once enacted, it cannot be amended by the state legislature. Instead, any amendments generally must be made through other initiatives. Practically speaking, that means it can be very difficult to amend ballot initiatives once they are voted into law.

There are a couple of other things that it is helpful to understand about the California legislative process. Firstly there are two legislative houses, the Senate and the Assembly. Member of either house can author a bill and the bills prefix indicates its house of origin i.e. AB or SB. But an author cannot simply draft a bill and put it to a vote the next day. Bills must pass through an orderly and predictable legislative process of introduction, printing, committee, 2nd and 3rd reading etc., before going through the whole process once more in the other legislative house. In order to soothe the bill's passage through the voting process it can be amended at any time but it must go back to its house of origin for concurrence. Although the purpose of these requirements is to provide the public with an opportunity to know and comment on pending changes in the law, the legislature has frequently bypassed these requirements by hijacking a bill at the tail end of a session, gutting it and amending it with an entirely new text. The gut and amend technique is often used when a bill is controversial or likely to generate significant opposition. Obviously, the practitioners of the gut and amend have no regard for transparency or public input. However sometimes it may be considered essential in passing essential bills – more of that later. For the time being it is of interest to know and keep in mind as the naming of the bills authored by both Mactaggart's Californians for Consumer Privacy and the state legislator's bill are both typically and very confusingly referred to as the California Consumer Privacy Act or CCPA despite them being completely separate bills.

The Timeline

If the genesis of the California Consumer Privacy Act – 2018 was novel in its approach in attempting to take the ballot to a state wide vote then its subsequent early development is quite baffling drama. The confusion arises primarily due to two bills proposed by different parties being introduced under the title of California Consumer Privacy Act. The original CCPA was first introduced in the California legislature in February 2017 but as a totally separate and much earlier bill than Alastair Mactaggart's ballot initiative of the same name. This early version of CCPA or as it was more commonly known as AB 375 was focused on cable and Internet service companies because Congress and the Trump administration effectively halted a set of federal consumer privacy protection rules on Internet service providers that were scheduled to take effect.

After a series of committee reviews and amendments in April, June and September, the emphasis on cable and internet service companies lessened and the AB 375 was moved to the inactive file on September 16, 2017. But keep this in mind as it is not the last we will hear of the AB 375 bill.

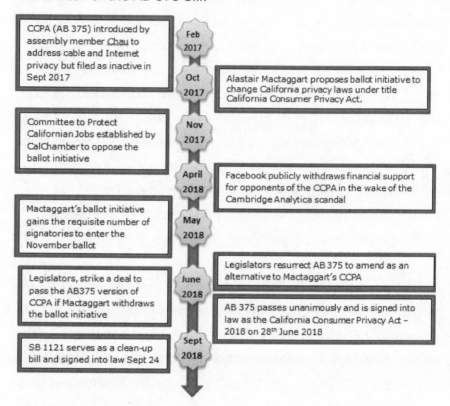

Approximately one month later a ballot initiative titled "The California Consumer Right to Privacy Act of 2018" ("Ballot Initiative") was filed with the California Attorney General on October 12, 2017. The stated purpose of the Ballot Initiative was to "give [Californians] important new consumer privacy rights to take back control of [their] personal information."

Alastair Mactaggart - chair of the group Californians for Consumer Privacy, sponsored the ballot initiative that would have circumvented the legislature and put the California Consumer Right to Privacy Act to a state wide vote in November.

With consumer privacy in mind, his team worked to develop a privacy initiative focusing on three pillars; transparency, control and accountability. These three principles form the basis of the ballot initiative created by Californians for Consumer Privacy, the California Consumer Privacy Act (CCPA). Overall, this act provides consumers with three fundamental rights:

1. The right to know what personal information is being collected;

2. The right to know what personal information is being sold and/or shared with third parties as well as the identity of those third parties; and

3. The right to request that their personal information no longer be sold (i.e., the right to opt out).

For the avoidance of confusion we refer to Mactaggart's CCPA bill as the Ballot Initiative. The ballot initiative was opposed, unsurprisingly, by a coalition of businesses called "Committee to Protect California Jobs," which characterized the Ballot Initiative as "limiting [our] choices, hurting [our] businesses, and cutting [our] connection to the global economy."

The following is the statement of Andrea Deveau of TechNet, Robert Callahan of the Internet Association, and Allan Zaremberg of the Chamber of Commerce, leaders of the Committee to Protect California Jobs, on the submission of signatures to qualify a ballot measure that calls for the California-only regulation of the Internet.

"This ballot measure disconnects California. It is unworkable, requiring the internet and businesses in California to operate differently than the rest of the world -- limiting our choices, hurting our businesses, and cutting our connection to the global economy."

"The internet is a seamless and global network. Yet the proponent, a multi-millionaire real estate developer with no background in privacy regulation, is seeking to create a California-only regulatory scheme. It makes no sense to attempt to wall off our state cutting off Californians from convenient services."

"The only real beneficiaries of this measure will be trial lawyers, who will be allowed to sue businesses for violation of the measure even if they cannot prove anyone has been harmed. This will open the floodgates for abusive, costly lawsuits."

"A broad-based coalition of businesses and organizations already opposes this poorly written, misguided proposal. We are confident that when the voters are educated on the true motivations and impacts of this ballot measure they will agree it is bad for California."

The Ballot Initiative reaches its target

By May 3, 2018, proponents of the Ballot Initiative announced that they had surpassed the requisite number of signatures to add the Ballot Initiative to California's November 2018 state-wide general election. The ballot initiative received 625,000 signatures, which is almost twice the number required for an initiative to be included on the California ballot.

In June according to the county registrars, sufficient numbers of signatures had been validated meaning that the California Consumer Privacy Act qualified for the November 2018 ballot. This certainly seems to have vindicated the approach taken by Alastair Mactaggart's Californians for Consumer Privacy and all their efforts in canvasing public support. Indeed as Alastair Mactaggart, says, with regards using the ballot to circumvent the legislative process, "It is doubtful that any state or federal legislature can pass a meaningful privacy law, given the amount of money tech companies and other players can throw at opposing such a bill. They probably think they can crush (opponents) like bugs and make the issue go away for several more years."

However, the ballot strategy would not be cheap as according to Ballotpedia, Alastair Mactaggart, had already personally donated $2.35 million in cash and services to support the initiative but a lot more would be required to fight a state ballot vote. In 2016, for example, ballot measure campaigns received approximately $1 billion overall, with more than $616 million going to support campaigns and $396 million to opposition campaigns.

Indeed the opposition — the Committee to Protect California Jobs — had already received over $1 million. But now that they were committed to fighting a state election the Committee to Protect Californians Jobs were expected to raise a $100m plus war-chest to contest the November ballot.

Steven Maviglio, spokesman for the Committee to Protect California Jobs and a political consultant, told Government Technology that the authors of the privacy initiative had not consider the "workability" of the measure and that it is almost impossible for organizations to comply with it.

However just as it appeared that the huge tech companies would ramp up their support on the side of the opposition doubts started to surface as Amazon, Google and Facebook took a backseat preferring to leave the lobbying to industry and trade associations such as The Internet Association and TechNet. For example, although Facebook initially contributed $200,000 to the Committee to Protect California Jobs, the social media giant in April 2018 announced it would stop providing funds to the opposition campaign and seek ways to focus its efforts on "supporting reasonable privacy measures in California," according to a National Public Radio (NPR) report.

Others such as Amazon and Google were extremely wary of being seen to be anti-privacy let alone seen to actively contest a consumers' privacy initiative as it could have serious negative impact on their brands. This concern was well founded due to requirement of California campaign finance law, which mandates that the largest donors to a campaign are listed at the end of each advertisement. Though Silicon Valley firms have the most to lose from the enactment of the CCPA, brand names such as Google and Amazon are wisely nervous to have their logos associated with a slash and burn election effort in opposition to consumer privacy rights.

Consequently, the tech and cable firms opposed to the bill have leaned heavily on their respective trade associations such as TechNet to head off the initiative. Perhaps taken aback by the level of support for the ballot initiative and the untimely surfacing of the Facebook-Cambridge Analytica debacle and Google's own undeclared exposure, they and Facebook were understandably unwilling to be seen to be taking sides in the ballot. Indeed both issued statements that distanced themselves from the opposition or at least publicly.

The real problem though was that despite their protestations to the contrary the largest technology and telecommunications firms were determined to derail the initiative as they are naturally inclined to do in response to all regulatory initiatives. Emails obtained by The Intercept revealed that the tech giants were still fighting behind the scenes to water down the privacy legislation, hoping to prevent an expensive and potentially damaging ballot fight in November.

Moreover, the tech giants were determined to derail the initiative as should it make it into law via the ballot-box it would be extremely difficult to change or repeal at a later date. This is because a ballot initiative can only be changed or repealed through a super majority of 70% in both legislative houses or by a subsequent ballot initiative going before the people. The trouble was the opponents to the bill only had three days to prevent the California Consumer Privacy Act, or CCPA, a ballot initiative that would usher in the strongest consumer privacy standards in the country, from going before state voters in November.

The return of AB 375

The idea that Californians might support the ballot and vote for these new privacy rights had spooked Silicon Valley, internet service providers, and many other industries that increasingly rely on data collection. However, if the tech companies were to be able to dilute the bill and gut many of the articles they disliked – for example the bill allowed consumers to opt out of the sale and collection of their personal data. It also vastly expanded the definition of personal information to include geolocation, biometrics, and browsing history. But most worrying was the initiative also allows consumers to pursue legal action for violations of the law. They would need to get the bill discussed via the legislative process and not the ballot-box. This inspired them to conduct intensive lobbying in the hope that they could somehow defeat the ballot initiative before it gained further traction.

At the same time or perhaps as a result of the intense lobbying the state legislators had become concerned with the prospect of such an important and far-reaching bill being passed via the ballot box rather than through due legislative process. This was understandably a major concern but they knew their best hope was to somehow convince the sponsors of the ballot initiative, including San Francisco real estate developer Alastair Mactaggart, to pull the proposal in exchange for some sort of compromise privacy legislation. The alternative privacy bill they proposed was the revised AB 375, which would achieve many but crucially not all of the same goals of the ballot initiative. In return the lawmakers behind the legislation, led by state Assembly Member Ed and Chair of the Assembly Committee on Privacy and Consumer Protection, Ed Chau, D-Monterey Park, and state Sen. Robert Hertzberg, D-Van Nuys, promised to swiftly pass the AB-375 bill if the sponsors of the ballot initiative withdrew the CCPA Ballot Initiative from the November ballot.

The motivation for the lawmakers to obtain a deal with Alastair Mactaggart, and the Californians for Consumer Privacy was clear. They did not want such an important bill going through the ballot and circumventing legislative scrutiny. Furthermore, the bill's passage into law taking this route would make it very difficult to change or repeal. However for the Californians for Consumer Privacy the benefits of a deal were less clear. They had after all already got the ballot initiative onto the November public election and should they ride the wave of popular support they could well win. The trouble was winning was not certain when up against the vast resources of the tech industry and their ad-hoc coalition of 40 odd local business allies. It was after all speculated that the opposition would have a war chest of around $110m as well as very broad support across Silicon Valley, commerce and business as shown by the diversity of companies within the business coalition. But time was on Mactaggart's side as the lawmakers had only three days to come up with a compromise deal. This meant that if the lawmaker's did want a deal they wouldn't be able to deploy stalling or hard ball tactics. After all the tables were now turned as it would be Silicon Valley and their cohorts who would be faced with a take it or leave it decision. The huge danger however was that once they agreed a compromise and pulled their bill from the ballot they would be effectively out of the game and watching from the side lines. It would then be down to the lawmakers to ensure that the bill passed through both houses without being effectively gutted by the fierce tech industry lobby groups.

Consequently, after eight months as an inactive file, CCPA (AB 375) was resurrected on June 21, 2018, gutted and amended so to speed up its journey through the legislative process as well. AB 375 has a final provision added that it only would take effect if the Ballot Initiative were withdrawn. As agreed the Ballot Initiative's proponents agreed to withdraw the Ballot Initiative should a compromise AB 375 be passed into law by June 29th 2018. Alastair Mactaggart agrees to work on the compromise based upon the restored AB 375 bill that would keep his initiative off the November ballot but to all purposes alive and well under the guise of AB 375. As a result, he and other interested parties, along with state lawmakers, draft a new bill based upon Assembly Bill 375

(AB 375). The newly amended AB 375 bill varies in certain areas from the original CCPA ballot initiative proposed by Mactaggart but still gives consumers certain rights to protect their data and requires businesses to develop and implement various policies and procedures to comply. The deal was that if the AB 375 was passed and signed by the California Governor by June 29, 2018, Alastair Mactaggart would withdraw his ballot initiative bill from the November ballot.

Meanwhile on the other side of the divide TechNet a trade group for Google, Facebook, and other tech companies, had been at the forefront of an ad-hoc business lobbying coalition formed to defeat the CCPA in any shape or form. In her email to the ad-hoc business coalition, Deveau a lobbyist for TechNet noted that AB 375 was moving fast, and that changes to the legislation would have to happen quickly over the coming days. If substantial changes were not made, she encouraged the lobbyists to prepare to begin raising cash for a pricey campaign over CCPA at the ballot box in November.

"In the meantime, you should assume that we are going to the ballot to fight the Initiative and determine your appetite or the appetite of your clients/members to fight the ballot initiative (meaning push hard to get a sense of how much you/they might be willing to contribute to the opposition campaign) if they feel they cannot live with this new language," Deveau warned.

The powerful lobbying coalition convened by Deveau over email includes Ryan Harkins, director of state affairs and public policy at Microsoft; Walter Hughes, the state director of government affairs at Comcast; Mufaddal Ezzy, the California manager of public policy and government relations for Google; Ann Blackwood, the head of public policy for western states at Facebook; Lisa Kohn, the senior manager for public policy at Amazon; Curt Augustine, the senior director of policy and government affairs for the Alliance of Automobile Manufacturers; Brad Weltman, the vice president for public policy at the Interactive Advertising Bureau; and Kate Ijams, a public affairs specialist at AT&T.

The inclusion of a Facebook representative is most notable, given the company's well-publicized announcement in the spring that it would end its opposition to the initiative. The firm, however, has maintained its promise not to pledge new money to the opposition effort. Nonetheless, Facebook is still in the loop when it comes to developing strategy about ways to undermine the CCPA. Interestingly, Facebook still takes a more pragmatic public stance where it unambiguously confirms support for the bill but at the same time is still in the loop for on-going involvement fighting CCPA. "People should be in control of their information online and companies should be held to high standards in explaining what data they have and how they use it, especially when they sell data," read a statement provided to The Intercept and attributed to Will Castleberry, Facebook's vice president of state and local public policy. "We are committed to being clear with people about how our services work, including the fact that we do not sell people's data. In that spirit, while not perfect, we support AB375 and look forward to working with policymakers on an approach that protects consumers and promotes responsible innovation."

In addition to Facebook, Google, AT&T, Microsoft, Amazon, Verizon, and the California New Car Dealers Association have each contributed six figure donations to the Chamber of Commerce account set up to defeat CCPA. Also, Uber, the Data & Marketing

Association, Cox Communications, and the Interactive Advertising Bureau have each contributed $50,000 to the account, according to disclosures. Certainly, it appears that fighting funds will not be an issue for the opponents of the CCPA. But the far trickier issue is balancing the defence of their business models against the PR damage incurred by showing contempt for their customer's rights to privacy.

Against this backdrop the revised AB 375 bill was crafted behind closed doors by the lawmakers, their sponsors and lobbyists, and when it was released it met with mix reception. It pleased some privacy advocates as a decent compromise that still provides strong new protections for consumers. For example the Consumer Watchdog, a consumer advocacy group, endorsed the new AB 375 legislation, calling it an agreement that enacts "meaningful privacy protections" while avoiding a costly ballot initiative battle. "If the initiative ends up on the ballot, Consumer Watchdog will work for its passage. Now, however, we support the AB 375 compromise," declared John Simpson, director of the group's Privacy and Technology Project.

But not everyone was so impressed for as the new bill was officially unveiled the tech lobby coalition joined other industry groups in Sacramento to express their concerns that the revised AB 375 bill still provided too many risks for business. The result of their efforts was the "compilation of feedback re: the most problematic aspects of AB 375." Within this document listed a vast array of issues lobbyists objected to, including a rewrite of the privacy law's description of what counts as personal information, changes to the conditions under which a consumer can seek legal action, the preservation of arbitration clauses in consumer contracts, and the removal of the mandate that firms display a button on their homepage giving consumers a clear way of opting out of data collection, amongst a raft of other changes.

The Chamber of Commerce were also appalled, "The business community is in an untenable situation. Although AB 375 is deeply flawed, the privacy initiative is even worse. The stakes are astronomical because if the initiative is passed, the legislature will be virtually unable to amend the law in the future," said Sarah Boot, a lobbyist with the California Chamber of Commerce and the first person to testify in opposition to the legislation at the Senate Judiciary Committee, which in turn is the first committee to oversee the compromise legislation.

After Boot spoke, a procession of likeminded lobbyists stepped up to the dais to register their disapproval and agree with Boot. Notably not a single tech company executive or their lobbyists appeared publicly, but multiple trade groups representing Silicon Valley spoke up to associate themselves with Boot's remarks. TechNet's Deveau, along with representatives of the Internet Association and the Computing Technology Industry Association, agreed that they deeply opposed AB 375, but found the legislation preferable over Mactaggart's ballot initiative.

"Here we are, at the last minute, there's an initiative on the ballot," said state Sen. Hannah-Beth Jackson, D-Santa Barbara, the chair of the committee, conceding that although the initiative was far from ideal, the issue had been forced because the legislature had not moved on any major privacy legislation. "Somebody stepped forward and now we are in a Hobson's choice. Either this goes to the ballot and is a hundred million dollars or more I'm told is likely to be spent. Or if the bill is killed we're back at ground zero," Jackson said with a sigh.

After a brief debate, with Chair of the Assembly Committee on Privacy and Consumer Protection, Ed Chau and the Chair of the Californians for Consumer Privacy, Alastair Mactaggart, answering questions about the bill, the committee unanimously passed the legislation and California Consumer Privacy Act 2018 (AB 375) on June 28th 2018 passed into law.

What is the AB 375 bill?

The new bill, which is an amendment to Assembly Bill 375 (AB 375), provides similar rights to consumers to protect their personal data, but it also brings important differences from the original ballot initiative. AB 375 provides the following rights to consumers:

- The right to know what personal information is collected;
- The right to know whether their personal information is sold or disclosed and to whom;
- The right to opt out of the sale of their personal information;
- The right to access their personal information;
- The right to request the deletion of their personal information; and
- The right to equal service and price, regardless of whether they exercise their privacy rights.

On June 28, 2018, California lawmakers enacted the California Consumer Privacy Act of 2018 (the "CCPA") a sweeping, GDPR-like privacy law which is intended to give California consumers more control over how businesses collect and use their data.

The new law is set to take effect on January 1, 2020 which means the California legislature may still consider changes to the new law in the coming months and years. Lawmakers moved swiftly to pass the bill to pre-empt a November ballot initiative that would have codified more stringent rules.

Hence the AB 375 may read like a fait accompli for the lawmakers and the Californians for Consumer Privacy against the tech companies and their ad hoc coalition aligned under the Chamber of Commerce but things are not always as they seem. Indeed from the perspective of tech companies and their allies the AB 375 is probably viewed more as a godsend than a catastrophe as now they have the time to lobby and apply their vast resources to effectively gutting the law. Hence accepting the AB 375 is more a means to buy time and the opportunity to assist in moulding its final form. It was for this reason that the bill passed unanimously. If it hadn't, the issue would have been deferred to a ballot initiative (CCPA) in November. Given that the latter could prove hugely expensive in terms of brand image to California's most important companies the revised AB 375 version of the CCPA is a fair and welcome compromise.

In essence the AB 375 is about:

- Allowing Californians to ask the three Ws in relation to their data: "what do you collect/store?", "why?", and "with whom do you share it?"
- It allows Californians to opt out of the sale of their personal data.
- It allows Californians to request deletion of their data.

That something like this would pass eventually was viewed by insiders as a fait accompli. The fallout from the many Facebook disclosures was too widespread, and the advent of measures like the EU's GDPR gave too compelling a blueprint.

What the AB 375 toned down or removed from the original Ballot Initiative were things like:

- The right for Californians to sue companies directly for data misuse and rule infringement.
- The inclusion of a highly visible "Don't Sell My Data" homepage button.
- The right for Californians to still receive services at the same price and quality after clicking opting out.
- Restrictions on how personal data could be used for ads (e.g., customer data could no longer be assembled into "profiles").

But the real issue wasn't just that the CCPA was viewed as too restrictive. It was that it contained a rider that made it very, very difficult to modify or overturn. If passed, it could only be undone by two-thirds of the popular vote (or else modified by a 70% vote from both state houses).

For obvious reasons, tech companies weren't going to go gently but even from their perspective the inconvenient truth was that the negative effect to their brands contesting a slash and burn campaign against effectively their own customers at the ballot-box would be hugely damaging.

That was why when the authors of CCPA agreed to pull their initiative off the table if the legislature would pass the AB 375 into law beforehand the tech industry fell in line in begrudging support. The tech companies realised that given the upside of at least having a chance to shape said legislation during 2019 was preferable to going to the ballot-box. Indeed, many industry players preferred this legislative approach over the now-abandoned ballot initiative. This was simply because now that the law had been passed they could expect a fuller review of the law's impact and more conversations about consumer protection and privacy rights in the US.

While the CCPA incorporates most of the ballot measure's major provisions and adopts similar types of requirements as we saw under GDPR, there are notable differences in several key areas. Here are our ten takeaways:

Covered entities: Far more entities are covered under the CCPA than under the ballot measure, as the new law applies to businesses that collect information from California residents and meet at least one of the following thresholds: (1) have over $25 million in annual gross revenue; (2) buy, receive, sell, or share for commercial purposes the personal information of 50,000 or more consumers, households, or devices; or (3) derive 50 percent or more of their revenue from the sale of consumers' personal information. The law is enforceable in California and applies to California users, but given the nature of data processing, most companies will need to consider whether to apply the rules to all users.

Disclosure requirements: At or before the point of collection, businesses must inform consumers the categories and specific pieces of personal information collected about the consumer, the sources from which that information is collected, the purpose for collecting or selling such personal information, the categories of personal information sold, and the categories of third parties to whom the personal information is shared. It also requires a description of consumers' rights and the categories of personal information the business has sold in the preceding 12 months.

Consumer access and data portability rights: Businesses that receive verifiable consumer requests must promptly take steps to disclose and deliver, free of charge to the consumer, the personal information requested by the consumer. The information may be delivered by mail or electronically, and if provided electronically, the information shall be in a portable and, to the extent technically feasible, in a readily useable format that allows the consumer to easily transmit this information to another entity. Businesses must provide consumers with two or more ways for submitting requests for information under the mandated disclosure provisions, including, at a minimum, a toll-free telephone number and a website address if the business has a website. The required information must be delivered within 45 days of receiving the request from the consumer.

Right to opt-out of data sharing: Consumers will have the right to direct businesses to stop selling their information to third parties. In order to comply with this "opt-out," business must conspicuously post their privacy policies as well as a link titled "Do Not Sell My Personal Information." The link must provide consumers with an easy mechanism that directs businesses to stop selling their information.

Right to be forgotten: Individuals will be able to direct Covered Entities to delete their personal information. Similar to GDPR, the law does contain some exceptions, including: information necessary to complete transactions; detect security breaches; protect against illegal activity; or to enable internal uses that are reasonably aligned with the expectations of the consumer based on the consumer's relationship with the business.

Right to opt in for children: The law also imposes new requirements on the sharing of personal information for children under the age of 16, effectively raising the age from the nationally recognized age of 13 which was set by the Children's Online Privacy Protection Act ("COPPA"). Covered Entities are prohibited from selling information about consumers between the ages of 13 and 16 without the consumers' explicit consent (opt-in) and must obtain parental consent before selling information about a consumer under the age of 13.

Expanded definition of "personal information": Personal Information includes not only traditional forms of personally identifiable information, but also IP addresses, geolocation, and "unique identifiers" such as device IDs, cookie IDs, and Internet activity information including browsing history and search history. Inferences drawn from the types of information described above "to create a profile about a consumer reflecting the consumer's preferences, characteristics, psychological trends, preferences, predispositions, behaviour, attitudes, intelligence, abilities, and aptitudes" are also included under the definition of personal information, similar to the definition of 'profiling' under GDPR which restricts the use of personal data to analyse or predict aspects a person's personal preferences, interests, reliability, behaviour, location or movements. The new right to access and deletion in California would be extended to these data categories.

Private actions: Unlike the ballot measure, the CCPA significantly limits private actions by giving the state Attorney General exclusive power to enforce the law, except in data breach cases where the Attorney General declines to prosecute within 30 days of being notified of a consumer's intent to bring suit. Even where a consumer is allowed to proceed with an action, they must give companies 30 days' written notice and an opportunity to "cure" the noticed violation within that time period. Similarly, businesses will have 30 days to cure any violations after receiving notice of noncompliance from the state Attorney General.

Damages: The CCPA also provides for damages in data breach cases to $750 per consumer per incident. In proceedings instituted by the Attorney General, entities that are found to have intentionally violated the law can face penalties of up to $7,500 per violation.

Prohibited practices: Businesses are prohibited from discriminating against consumers that exercise their rights under the law. Specifically, businesses cannot deny consumers goods or services, charge consumers different prices or rates (or otherwise impose a penalty), or provide consumers a different quality or level of goods or services. A business can, however, provide consumers with "financial incentives," including compensation, for allowing the business to collect, sell, or not delete consumers' personal information.

While the CCPA is somewhat more business-friendly than its sister ballot measure, it nonetheless gives consumers unprecedented control over their personal information and creates new and onerous challenges for companies that do business in California. While the new law purports to reduce litigation by limiting private actions, businesses should still brace themselves for an active enforcement climate. For now, it looks like companies that restructured their operations to comply with GDPR will have to expand their efforts for California. And given the high likelihood that other states will follow suit, it is likely we will see a wave of GDPR-like activity in the United States ahead of that 2020 deadline.

Chapter 3 – Who are the major players

In the last 12 months, data privacy has moved from a niche topic to something talked about at almost every corporation's board meeting. The emergence of the EU GDPR, which came into force on May 25th, 2018, covers data held on any EU citizen and enforced new accountability for organizations processing personal data. With the legislature passing the California Consumer Privacy Act 2018 (AB 375) on June 29th 2018, there are now a similar set of rules governing most organisations holding data on US Citizens.

California has passed a landmark privacy bill that restricts the data-harvesting practices of technology companies like Facebook, Google and Amazon and gives consumers more control over their personal information.

The California Consumer Privacy Act is designed to provide new protections to the state's 40 million residents in the wake of major privacy breaches including the Cambridge Analytica scandal.

The new rules give Californians the right to see what information is being collected about them and to request that data be deleted, to find out whether their information is being sold to third parties including advertisers and to request that they stop doing so.

Nonetheless, none of these privacy rights could possibly have come to fruition without some major activity on behalf of the consumer. After all federal and state laws have previously floundered no matter how well intentioned they started out being due to intensive lobbying from the huge technology businesses and consequently the major dilution of pertinent principles that rendered them void of purpose. However, in California, the very home of many of these technology behemoths the proponents of consumer privacy have claimed a major victory in establishing laws that protect the rights of privacy for Californians. So who are the organisations that have proposed sponsored and fought for the rights of the consumer?

Californians for Consumer Privacy

The Californians for Privacy group is a coalition of like-minded individuals and organisations under the chair of Alastair Mactaggart, the improbable but indefatigable champion of the California Consumer Privacy Act. Their stated mantra, "Your life is not their business", is a carefully crafted warning to Californians to beware of businesses that profit from harvesting peoples personal information and despite what the tech industry may insinuate the two are not connected.

As Alastair Mactaggart, tells it, "After two years of research, we drafted an initiative based on three principles: transparency, control and accountability.

"Transparency: we should be able to know what personal information companies collect about us, our children and our devices, and who they are selling it to.

"Control: consumers should be able to tell companies not to sell their personal information, and companies shouldn't be able to retaliate against consumers who exercise this choice.

"Accountability: after all the massive data breaches in the last few years, whether at Facebook, Target, Equifax or Yahoo, it became glaringly apparent that many of these big companies don't care enough about your data security. We drafted the initiative to hold them more accountable if they fail to take good care of your personal information.

"In the final analysis, it seemed to us that since we already pay our cell phone and cable bills, our auto leases and music subscription services, shouldn't we be able to tell those companies that they can't also sell the personal information they obtain from us as users and customers? And as for 'free' services—well, as the saying goes, if you're not paying for the product, you are the product."

The Californians for Consumer Privacy have driven the privacy ballot initiative and are made up of a number of coalition members of which Mozilla, Privacy Rights Clearinghouse, CALPIRG, the Center for Public Interest Law, Oakland Police Officers Association, Parent Coalition for Student Privacy, Disconnect, and the Academy of Integrated Health and Medicine, amongst others. As of June 28, 2018, Californians for Consumer Privacy had raised $3.05 million, with 98.4 percent of funds coming from Alastair Mactaggart. Although undoubtedly the major coalition driving the bill for consumer privacy in California there are other significant groups dedicated to consumer privacy that are playing a supporting role.

Common Sense Kids

Common Sense Kids Action is committed to equipping parents, educators, and policymakers with the tools to fight for state and federal policy changes. They are advocates for legislation that protects kids and allows them to thrive safely in the digital age.

"The Consumer Privacy Act will allow consumers to take control of and make informed choices about their own data, control that fosters a healthy relationship to technology and overall digital wellbeing," said Elizabeth Galicia, from Common Sense Media, which co-sponsored the bill.

"Kids are the most tracked generation ever. Their personal information, activities and networks are exposed and often for sale from birth. This law is a strong first step in protecting kids and all consumers," she added.

Electronic Frontier Foundation

The Electronic Frontier Foundation is a leading non-profit organization committed to defending civil liberties in the digital world. Founded in 1990, EFF champions user privacy, free expression, and innovation through impact litigation, policy analysis, grassroots activism, and technology development.

The EFF believes the California Consumer Privacy Act is a well-intentioned but flawed new law that seeks to protect the data privacy of technology users and others by imposing new rules on companies that gather, use, and share personal data. The EFF finds that there is a lot to like about the Act, but there is substantial room for improvement. Most significantly they would like to have opt-in rather than the weaker opt-out when users provide consent. They would also take a stronger line on the users' rights to take violators to court.

Privacy Rights Clearinghouse

Since 1992, Privacy Rights Clearinghouse has empowered individuals to protect their privacy by providing direct one-to-one assistance, creating original educational publications, and advocating for consumer-friendly policy. PRC believes that California could take the lead again by passing into law the California Consumer Privacy Act of 2018 (AB 375), a bill that alters the state's privacy landscape. This bill would bring a much-needed expansion of consumer privacy protections by giving us more control over how consumer personal information is used and shared. The PRC say that they do, "recognize that it's not perfect, but AB 375 would take a meaningful step towards providing the kinds of crucial protections that we need and demand. During a time with massive violations of public trust from Equifax to Facebook/Cambridge Analytica, California must take action to protect privacy for all Californians—which is why we are supporting this legislation."

Another highly influential supporter of the bill is Senator Bill Dodd, one of the bill's co-authors; "This bill will be the strongest of its kind in the nation and enact safeguards we need in the 21st century,

"Big data is big business. It's time we regulate it appropriately and hold bad actors accountable.

"It is critical going forward that policymakers work to correct the inevitable, negative policy and compliance ramifications this last-minute deal will create for California's consumers and businesses alike."

The Opponents

The passing of the law comes the month after Europe introduced similar sweeping privacy protections under the General Data Protection Regulation (GDPR). In Europe the GDPR gives individuals the right to demand companies reveal or delete the personal data they hold and regulators can work together across Europe for the first time, rather than launching separate actions in each country. It also introduces harsh penalties, with a maximum fine of €20m or 4% of the company's global turnover.

Similarly, when the CCPA comes into effect on 1 January 2020, companies could be penalised up to $7,500 for each intentional violation. The rules will be enforced by California's attorney general and of course this has not gone down well with the Chamber of Commerce and its members.

Chamber of Commerce (CalChamber)

The California Chamber of Commerce has its own team of California business advocates that maintains a steady presence at the State Capitol that gives their labour law experts front-line knowledge of new laws and regulations. That means that they are always among the first to know about any new laws that may affect local business and employees – and how to comply.

In fact, CalChamber is the leading advocate for California business at the State Capitol, at the ballot box, with regulatory agencies and in the courts. CalChamber is determined and committed to defeat unnecessary mandates to minimize the costs of doing business in California so that businesses can create jobs.

The initial coalition that was built to fight Alastair Mactaggart's original ballot Initiative on consumer privacy was the "Committee to Protect California Jobs," which characterized the Ballot Initiative as "limiting [our] choices, hurting [our] businesses, and cutting [our] connection to the global economy." As of June 28, 2018, the campaign had raised $2.15 million, with several electronic, telecommunications, and vehicle companies each giving $200,000. Companies including Amazon, AT&T, Comcast, Facebook, Google, Microsoft, Verizon, and Uber had donated to the campaign (although Facebook and Google have since –publicly at least - withdrawn their opposition to the bill) and the coalition are likely to spend the coming months lobbying to water-down the law.

A spokesperson for the tech-friendly group called the privacy act "flawed," and pointed out that while tech giants are opposed to the legislation, they're not the only ones. "Credit unions, grocers, and car manufacturers are among the many recent additions to the coalition and are the top of the iceberg," spokesperson Steven Maviglio noted. He added that the "workability" of the proposal is also problematic, saying, "no-one who orders anything from Amazon can request where their information went, and that can not only overwhelm a large company like Amazon but also smaller ones too."

Internet Association

The Internet Association is a trade coalition that exclusively represents leading global internet companies on matters of public policy. Their mission is to foster innovation, promote economic growth, and empower people through the free and open internet. With a membership boasting internet giants such Amazon, Google,

Facebook, LinkedIN, Twitter and eBay they claim to favour a privacy framework that is consistent nationwide, proportional, flexible, and should encourage companies to act as good stewards of the personal information provided to them by individuals. However they also insist that this policy framework is mindful of the impact of regulation on small- and medium-sized companies but at the same time they must meet individuals' reasonable expectations with respect to how the personal information they provide to companies will be collected, used, and shared.

Indeed, such is the Internet Associations commitment to consumer privacy they and their members are striving to create their own federal privacy policy. The Internet Association therefore does not look favourably upon state privacy policy and expressed concern over the speed with which the law was passed.

Internet Association Vice President of State Government Affairs Robert Callahan issued the following statement on the passage of the California Consumer Privacy Act – 2018 (AB 375) in California: "Data regulation policy is complex and impacts every sector of the economy, including the internet industry. That makes the lack of public discussion and process surrounding this far-reaching bill even more concerning. The circumstances of this bill are specific to California. It is critical going forward that policymakers work to correct the inevitable, negative policy and compliance ramifications this last-minute deal will create for California's consumers and businesses alike."

TechNet

TechNet is the national, bipartisan network of technology CEOs and senior executives that promotes the growth of the innovation economy by advocating a targeted policy agenda at the federal and 50-state level. Their membership consists of tech giants such as Amazon, Cisco, Facebook, Google, Microsoft, Uber and Visa.

"While this law adds a significant new layer of privacy protections for California consumers, even its authors have acknowledged it is far from perfect and will need revisions in the months ahead as its consequences and workability are better understood," said Linda Moore, president and CEO of the lobby group TechNet.

The Business Coalition

More than three dozen business groups from the tech, retail, health, banking and other sectors are pushing California lawmakers working on making "technical" changes to a hastily enacted landmark privacy law. Indeed the Committee to Protect Californian Jobs concurred claiming they had the support not just from tech companies but across diverse businesses such as credit unions, grocers, and car manufacturers are among the many recent additions to the coalition and are these are just the tip of the body of opposition.

Some of these diverse members who were signatories to the letter sent to the lawmakers requesting changes during the clean-up process (SB 1211) are listed below;

California Chamber of Commerce
Advanced Medical Technology Association
Alliance of Automobile Manufacturers
American Council of Life Insurers
American Insurance Association
Association of California Life & Health Insurance Companies

Association of National Advertisers

California Bankers Association

California Business Properties Association

California Cable & Telecommunications Association

California Community Banking Network

California Credit Union League

California Financial Services Association

California Hospital Association

California Land Title Association

California Life Sciences Association

California Manufacturers & Technology Association

California Mortgage Bankers Association

California Retailers Association

CompTIA

Consumer Data Industry Association

Consumer Technology Association

CTIA

Delta Dental

Interactive Advertising Bureau

International Pharmaceutical & Medical Privacy
Consortium

Internet Association

Internet Coalition

Motion Picture Association of America

National Association of Insurance and Financial Advisors

National Business Coalition on E-Commerce and Privacy

NetChoice

Pacific Association of Domestic Insurance Companies

Personal Insurance Federation of California

Retail Industry Leaders Association

Securities Industry and Financial Markets Association

Software and Information Industry Association

TechNet

The California Consumer Privacy Act of 2018 (the "Act") was signed into law by California Governor Jerry Brown on June 28, 2018, after being hastily introduced in the California Legislature just a few days prior. The bill was introduced in response to a coming together of events concerning consumers' personal information, such as the failure of federal or state legislature to come up with a viable privacy act; the failure of the tech and advertising industries to self-regulate; heightened public awareness of poor data privacy regulations due to the Facebook/Cambridge Analytica scandal; and a California ballot initiative that qualified for the November ballot and proposed the California Consumer Privacy Act ("CCPA Initiative"). As a result, the legislature in California responded with AB-375, which proposed an alternative version of the CCPA Initiative which would circumvent the costs and risks involved in a state-wide ballot. The authors of AB-375 worked out a compromise with the sponsors of the CCPA Initiative, and subsequently a revised AB-375 was passed and signed by Governor Jerry Brown, becoming the California Consumer Privacy Act of 2018, codified at Title 18.1.5 of the California Civil Code (the "CCPA").

Brief History on California Privacy Laws

To help understand how California arrived at its new privacy act the CCPA, which takes effect in January of 2020, it is helpful to revisit the privacy-legislation history over the last 45-plus years. The fact that California is at the forefront of new consumer privacy laws is hardly surprising given their record for pioneering privacy bills. For it was way back in 1972 that California voted to include the right of privacy among the "inalienable" rights of all people. That right gave individuals the ability to control the use, including the sale, of their personal information. The state followed with adopting privacy measures that include:

• Online Privacy Protection Act
• Privacy Rights for California Minors in the Digital World Act
• Shine the Light, a California law intended to give Californians the "who, what, where, and when" of how businesses handle consumers' personal information.

The problem is though that as pioneering as these laws were technology moves swiftly whereas legislature tends towards a more glacial pace. The California lawmakers in the California Consumer Privacy Act of 2018 recognised this inherent failure to keep up when they wrote in the bill that "California law has not kept pace with these developments and the personal privacy implications surrounding the collection, use, and protection of personal information." As an example of the latest threats to consumer privacy that current laws were insufficient to mitigate they cited the "devastating effects for individuals" with loss of privacy and the "misuse" of data by Cambridge Analytica. They expanded upon this by stating that in today's digital world, "California consumers should be able to exercise control over their personal information, and they want to be certain that there are safeguards against misuse of their personal information." In the lawmakers view, "It is possible for businesses both to respect consumers' privacy and provide a high level transparency to their business practices."

CCPA is consistent with California's history of actively protecting its residents' privacy rights. In 2004, the California Online Privacy Protection Act ("CalOPPA") came into effect as the first US state law, which required website operators to post privacy policies detailing their information handling processes. Similarly, CCPA like CalOPPA is focused on protecting California residents by requiring notice about a business's personal information management and practices. CCPA regulates an entity "that does business" in California and meets specified thresholds. CalOPPA is not limited to California businesses — CalOPPA applies to any operator of a "Web site located on the Internet or an online service" that collects and maintains personal information from a California resident who uses or visits the Web site or online service. Nonetheless, in effect CCPA's scope is significantly broader as it has a more expansive definition of personal information than CalOPPA and applies to a business covered by the act engaging in "collection and sale of all personal information" and not just personal information collected online. The AB 375 as a result of being revised so quickly does not repeal any of the prior laws instead it states that if there is conflict or ambiguity then the stricter of the respective provisions will apply.

CCPA – Relevant for the digital age

The California Constitution grants the right of privacy and existing law provides for the confidentiality of personal information in various contexts. These established laws requires a business or person that suffers a breach of security of computerized data that includes personal information, as defined, to disclose that breach, as specified. The purpose of the AB 375 is to update the law to ensure its relevance in the digital society.

- This bill would enact the California Consumer Privacy Act of 2018. Beginning January 1, 2020, the bill would grant a consumer a right to request a business to disclose the categories and specific pieces of personal information that it collects about the consumer, the categories of sources from which that information is collected, the business purposes for collecting or selling the information, and the categories of 3rd parties with which the information is shared.
- The bill would require a business to make disclosures about the information and the purposes for which it is used and it would grant a consumer the right to request deletion of personal information and would require the business to delete upon receipt of a verified request, as specified.
- The bill would grant a consumer a right to request that a business that sells the consumer's personal information, or discloses it for a business purpose, disclose the categories of information that it collects and categories of information and the identity of 3rd parties to which the information was sold or disclosed.
- The bill would require a business to provide this information in response to a verifiable consumer request.
- The bill would authorize a consumer to opt out of the sale of personal information by a business and would prohibit the business from discriminating against the consumer for exercising this right, including by charging the consumer who opts out a different price or providing the consumer a different quality of goods or services, except if the difference is reasonably related to value provided by the consumer's data.

- The bill would authorize businesses to offer financial incentives for collection of personal information. The bill would prohibit a business from selling the personal information of a consumer less than 16 years of age, unless affirmatively authorized, as specified, to be referred to as the right to opt in. The bill would prescribe requirements for receiving, processing, and satisfying these requests from consumers.

- The bill would prescribe various definitions for its purposes and would define "personal information" with reference to a broad list of characteristics and behaviours, personal and commercial, as well as inferences drawn from this information.

- The bill would prohibit the provisions described above from restricting the ability of the business to comply with federal, state, or local laws, among other things.

- The bill would provide for its enforcement by the Attorney General, as specified, and would provide a private right of action in connection with certain unauthorized access and exfiltration, theft, or disclosure of a consumer's non-encrypted or non-redacted personal information, as defined.

- The bill would prescribe a method for distribution of proceeds of Attorney General actions

- The bill would create the Consumer Privacy Fund in the General Fund with the moneys in the fund, upon appropriation by the Legislature, to be applied to support the purposes of the bill and its enforcement.

- The bill would provide for the deposit of penalty money into the fund. The bill would require the Attorney General to solicit public participation for the purpose of adopting regulations, as specified.

- The bill would authorize a business, service provider, or 3rd party to seek the Attorney General's opinion on how to comply with its provisions.
- The bill would void a waiver of a consumer's rights under its provisions.
- The bill would condition its operation on the withdrawal of a specified initiative from the ballot.

The last statement on the list solidified the agreement with Mactaggart that upon the passing of the bill that he would withdraw his ballot initiative. Hence it would only be upon the withdrawal of the ballot initiative that the act would come into operation.

The resultant California Consumer Privacy Act - 2018 is seen by some as preferable to the ballot initiative – although confusingly they had the same names - because it provides future-proof mechanisms to refine its privacy-related requirements, which makes it easier to amend the Act at a later date. However, as described below, that does not mean that compliance with the Act will be a quick and painless process; instead, it's likely that many companies will find the compliance process as much of a struggle as their GDPR compliance efforts.

The CCPA is often irreverently described as mini-GDPR but it also builds on existing data privacy legislation in California including the "Shine the Light" law, the California Online Privacy Protection Act, and California's data breach notification law. The CCPA was passed amid concerns that consumers cannot "properly protect and safeguard their privacy."

The introduction of the CCPA comes at a time when many US companies with international operations are still dealing with the GDPR and it considerable compliance burden in resources and finance. Nonetheless, despite some high-level conceptual similarities, the CCPA and the GDPR are dissimilar at the lower technical levels of compliance. Hence, the CCPA will not just fit snugly into the GDPR framework, far from it, and it will place additional burdens on businesses that are subject to both laws.

CCPA (Ballot) Vs. AB 375

The new Act the CCPA, which is an amendment to Assembly Bill 375 (AB 375), provides similar rights to consumers to protect their personal data, but also brings key differences from the original ballot initiative. AB 375 provides the following 6 principle privacy rights to consumers:

- The right to know what personal information is collected;
- The right to know whether their personal information is sold or disclosed and to whom;
- The right to opt-out of the sale of their personal information;
- The right to access their personal information;
- The right to request the deletion of their personal information; and
- The right to equal service and price, regardless if they exercise their privacy rights.

As originally proposed, in the Ballet Initiative, businesses will have 45 days to respond to consumer requests to exercise any of their rights. The key differences between the original CCPA and AB 375 are that AB 375 provides the additional right to deletion. But as it gives, it also takes away, for the AB 375 removes the provision for a private right of action against a business for any violation of the Act. Instead, AB 375 provides a more business-friendly approach whereby it provides businesses with more scope to limit penalty amounts. To this affect, businesses are provided a 30-day window to "cure" any alleged violations. What this means is that if the business can prove the violations have been "cured" and that no further violations will occur, the state attorney general will not be able to pursue legal action against them. An example, of curing a violation could be if a business does not delete information after a requester has gone through due process. This of course could be down to a technical issue – not knowing every location of the information – so the business will have 30 days to investigate and resolve the issues. However, should the business fix the issue within the 30 days and demonstrate that the violation cannot happen again then that would be considered a cure. But, should violators fail to comply and provide a cure within the allotted time then they are facing a maximum penalty of $7,500 per intentional violation. Finally, consumers are not provided with a private right of action for violations of the 6 principle rights listed above.

Whereas AB 375 removed the right of action for consumers against violations of the CCPA Act, it does provide amended rules regarding data breaches. Consumers are provided with a private right of action and can seek damages in the event of a breach where the business has failed to implement "reasonable security procedures and practices appropriate to the nature of the information to protect the personal information." Damages that occur as the result of a breach are limited to a maximum of $750 per consumer per incident.

Another embellishment is that interestingly the legislators increased the catchment range for AB 375 jurisdiction as it will apply different criteria for a covered business than the original CCPA. AB 375 as it is written now applies to any for-profit business that earns $25 million – down from $50m - in revenue per year, sells 50,000 consumer records – down from 100k per year, or derives 50% of its annual revenue from selling personal information. As with the CCPA, AB 375 applies to any business collecting or selling personal information from California regardless of the physical location of the business.

Businesses subject to the AB 375 bill will be required to implement various new policies and procedures ensuring the protection of personal information, including updates to privacy policies, "reasonable" security protections, and facilitation of consumer rights. Each request from consumers must be formally analysed as various scenarios may exist in which a business does not have to honour a consumer's request to exercise one of their rights.

Businesses covered by these requirements should begin to map out all personal information collected and shared from Californians at the earliest opportunity. A lesson learned from GDPR compliancy projects was that one of the more onerous tasks was actually identifying and locating all the personal information being stored by a business. This analysis should include the categories of personal information collected, why the information is collected, and to whom the information is shared or sold. This will allow businesses to more easily respond to consumer requests as businesses can probably expect a high number of requests initially. Lastly, businesses must determine how they will comply with this new regulation – will the business honour these rights on a nationwide basis or will the business implement a process to determine the location of the consumer making the request and only honour those requests coming from California? How will it determine this? It is likely this may well only be the first of many data protection laws to be enacted in the United States. Hence, companies should perhaps take a more extensive vision and prepare for additional state and maybe even federal changes to how businesses can handle personal data.

What is the CCPA's (AB 375) Scope: Covered Entities, "Personal Information" and "Consumers"

The CCPA – in this context and title refers to the California Consumer Privacy Act 2018 (AB 375) - applies to for-profit legal entities (or sole proprietorships) that:

(i) do business in the State of California;
(ii) collect personal information of consumers;
(iii) determine the purpose and means of the processing of consumers' personal information; and
(iv) either have annual gross revenue over $25,000,000; buy, sell, receive or share for commercial purposes, the personal information of 50,000 or more consumers, devices or households, on an annual basis; or derive 50 percent or more of their annual revenue from selling the personal information of consumers.

However a lot of the devil lies in the detail such as how some key-terms are precisely defined within the context of the act. For example, Personal Information is broadly defined as "information that identifies, relates to, describes, is capable of being associated with, or could reasonably be linked, directly or indirectly, with a particular consumer or household." The CCPA provides several examples of personal information, including real name, alias, IP address, biometric information, network activity information (e.g., browsing and search history), and geolocation data.

The CCPA applies to "consumers" which it defines as natural persons who are California residents. Although the CCPA references and appears designed to protect consumers in the commonly understood sense (i.e., recipients of a good or service), but that would for its purpose be to limiting hence its broader definition. This more expansive definition allows it to cover data obtained in other circumstances, such as personal data shared or bought for marketing or research purposes but it could also be related to a business's employees or next-of-kin who are California residents.

The CCPA specifically identifies "employment-related data" as a category of personal information covered by the CCPA and its legislative recitals do mention "apply[ing] for a job" as one of the activities that is "almost impossible to do ... without sharing personal information." Additionally, the CCPA never states that it applies only to personal information collected in the course of a consumer transaction as that would be too limited or expressly excludes personal information collected by an employer about its employees for employment purposes. The scope of the CCPA will likely need to be clarified through legislative amendment, regulation, or guidance from the AG.

Nonetheless, despite its potentially broad reach, the CCPA is not all encompassing. For example, the CCPA does not apply to "commercial conduct" which takes place entirely outside of California. In addition, the CCPA is not intended to replace or supersede federal and state laws. The 1121 bill used as a vehicle to clear-up some of the technical issues with AB 375 stipulated that the act did not apply to personal information collected pursuant to certain laws, such as the Health Insurance Portability and Accountability Act and the Gramm–Leach–Bliley Act. The CCPA also notably excludes "personal information" transferred as part of a merger, acquisition or other corporate transaction, subject to certain conditions. Notably, including requiring notice to a consumer if the acquirer of the information plans to use it in a way that is incompatible with the conditions under which it was originally collected.

Compliance Obligations

With regards compliance with the law the CCPA imposes substantial obligations on covered businesses:

Provide Prior Notice of Data Collection Practices: At the time of, or before collecting personal information, a business must inform consumers of the categories of personal information to be collected and the purpose for which each category of personal information will be used. However, this prior notice could be included in the business's external privacy policy.

Update Privacy Policy: A business should disclose (and update at least every 12 months) in both its existing privacy policy and any California-specific privacy description:

- a description of consumers' specific rights under the CCPA and the methods provided by the business for consumers to submit corresponding requests (including if the business sells personal information, a link to a "Do Not Sell My Personal Information" webpage).
- lists, in respect of the preceding 12 months, of:
  1. the categories of personal information collected, the sources from which such personal information was collected, the categories of third parties with whom such personal information was shared;
  2. the business or commercial purpose for collecting or selling personal information; and
  3. the categories of personal information disclosed (for a business purpose) or sold (or a statement that the business has not engaged in such sale or disclosure, if applicable).
- Honour Consumer Requests: A business is under an obligation to honour consumer rights granted under the CCPA within 45 days. The CCPA requires businesses to:
  1. Access: disclose the following, in relation to personal information it has collected about the consumer in the preceding twelve months:
     (a) the specific pieces of information collected;
     (b) the categories of information collected;
     (c) the categories of sources from which that information was collected;

(d) the business or commercial purpose for collecting that information; and

(e) the categories of third parties with whom that information has been shared, including information sold to third parties. The disclosure should be made in writing and delivered: through the consumer's account with the business, if they have one (if not they should not be asked to create one); by mail; or electronically, at the consumer's option if they do not have an account (in which case the information must be provided in a readily useable format that allows the consumer to easily transmit the information to another entity). Such requests are limited to two per twelve-month period.

- The business must provide at least two designated methods for consumers to submit requests, including, at a minimum, a toll-free telephone number and a web page (if the business maintains a web site).

The Right to be Forgotten: the right to delete the personal information the business has collected from the consumer, subject to certain exceptions, including if the consumer's personal information is necessary for the business or service provider to: (a) provide a good or service requested by the consumer; (b) complete the transaction for which personal information was collected; or (c) perform a contract between the business and consumer.

The Right to Opt-out: if they sell personal information to third parties, refrain from selling a consumer's personal information (and not request that the consumer authorize the sale of their personal information for at least twelve months from the opt-out).

The business must provide a clear and conspicuous link entitled "Do Not Sell My Personal Information" on its website that directs consumers to a webpage where they can opt-out.

Prohibited Discrimination: A business must not discriminate against a consumer who chooses to exercise his or her rights under the CCPA, e.g., by increasing prices, or reducing the level or quality of goods or services for those consumers. This does not prevent a business from varying prices, or the level or quality of goods or services if the difference equates to the value provided to the consumer by the consumer's data. Businesses may (1) offer financial incentives such as payments to a consumer as compensation, for the collection, sale, and deletion of personal information, and/or (2) offer a different price, rate, level, or quality of goods and services to consumers "if the difference is related to the value of having a consumer's personal information."

Educate Personnel: A business is under an obligation to ensure that individuals responsible for handling consumer inquiries about the business's privacy practices or the business's compliance with the CCPA are informed of all requirements, and how to direct consumers to exercise their rights.

Penalties

State Enforcement: The CCPA contains significant tools for enforcement. Violation of the CCPA would expose businesses to civil penalties of up to $7,500 per intentional violation in suits brought by the AG (or any other public entity with the authority to sue on the behalf of the people of California). Civil penalties for non-intentional violations will be limited to $2,500 or less per violation. Businesses will have 30 days to cure any alleged violations after being notified of non-compliance.

Consumer Actions: The CCPA grants a right for consumers to bring a civil action for statutory damages. However, this applies only in relation to data security breaches which arise out of a failure by a business to comply with its duty (under a separate law) to maintain reasonable data security measures. In this context, consumers whose unencrypted or non-redacted personal information (defined by that separate law, and more narrowly than in the remainder of the CCPA) has been stolen or disclosed as a result of a business's violation of its duty to implement and maintain reasonable security procedures and practices appropriate to the nature of the information. Statutory damages are the greater of $100-$750 per consumer per incident, and actual damages. As such, an applicable data breach, involving as little as 10,000 records, could subject a business to a million dollar plus damages claim.

Compliance in Practice: To be prepared in practice to comply with these obligations under the CCPA, businesses are likely to need to implement operational changes, for example so that, for a given California resident, they are able to identify all relevant personal information they hold, are able to provide a copy and/or delete it on request, and, to the extent they sell personal information, to refrain from selling that particular California resident's personal information.

CCPA – A work in progress

Before it takes effect on January 1, 2020, the CCPA calls for the AG to solicit public input in developing regulations and procedures for certain key provisions of the law. It is also likely to be revised by the California legislature during 2019. For example, the California legislature recently passed S.B. 1121, which makes several substantial changes to the CCPA. Along with the technical corrections, S.B. 1121 amends the CCPA to make clear that the private right of action only applies to data breaches. It also extends the deadline for the AG to issue regulations under the CCPA from January 1, 2020 to July 1, 2020 hence the CCPA would not now be enforceable until the earlier of July 1, 2020 or six months after the AG publishes final CCPA regulations.

Consequently, there are opportunities for businesses to raise concerns and objections and by doing so play a part in influencing its final form. To participate in the AG's proposed rulemaking process, participants will generally have 45 days from the date of announcement of the proposed rulemaking to submit their comments, either via email, fax, postal address, or at a public hearing. Businesses may also seek the advice of the AG on how to comply with the law and the AG will provide a means by which businesses may solicit such advice.

However, as AB 375 won't come into effect until January 2020, we can expect the following aspects of the law to be diluted by intensive lobbying from the tech and business sector:

- The list of what qualifies as personal data to be made narrower / more concrete.
- Direct suit options to be limited in lieu of funneling complaints through bodies like the California AG office.

(Some industry-requested changes were already reflected in AB 375, such as the downgraded placement of the "Don't Sell My Data" button and the diminished listing requirements for third-party data acquirers.)

Compatibility with the GDPR

For a global business, the CCPA will add an additional regulatory burden on top of the significant compliance overhead from other data privacy regimes, most notably the GDPR. Although certain provisions of the CCPA resemble at a conceptual level certain provisions of the GDPR, even those similar provisions also include subtle technical differences. Therefore, while, businesses may find that existing compliance frameworks developed under the GDPR are useful for preparing for compliance under the CCPA, this will not avoid the need for a review of and updates to these frameworks. For businesses that have already been through the rigours of the compliance demands of the GDPR roadmap having to revisit the conundrum from the perspective of the CCPA, once again and so soon will be disheartening.

Who has to comply with the Act?

The Act will apply to for-profit businesses that collect and control California residents' personal information, do business in the State of California, and: (a) have annual gross revenues in excess of $25 million; or (b) receive or disclose the personal information of 50,000 or more California residents, households or devices on an annual basis; or (c) derive 50 percent or more of their annual revenues from selling California residents' personal information. The Act also draws in corporate affiliates of such businesses that share their branding. That means that not-for-profits, small companies, and/or those that do not traffic in large amounts of personal information, and do not share a brand with an affiliate who is covered by the Act, will not have to comply with the Act.

A company also is exempted from its compliance obligations under the Act "if every aspect of ... commercial conduct takes place wholly outside of California," meaning that: (1) the business collected the information from the consumer in question while he or she was outside California, (2) no part of any sale of his or her personal information occurred in California, and (3) no personal information collected while the consumer was in California is sold. Realistically, though, many companies will remain subject to the Act by virtue of having "consumers" (California residents) among their customers.

Who is protected by the Act?

The Act requires that the protections listed above be made available to "consumers," who are defined as California residents for tax purposes. However, California's large population and economic presence means that many (if not most) companies serve California consumers – even if those companies have no physical presence in the State. Additionally, few companies are likely to cabin all of the Act's requirements to California residents, as it is difficult to offer a different Web site experience to residents of a specific state. For example, few companies are likely to devote the resources necessary to provide the Act's opt-out options to a user visiting a Web site from an IP address in California, while providing a Web site without those features to residents of the other 49 states. Realistically, this makes it likely that companies with California-based customers – which is most

U.S. companies that have an online presence – will need to comply with the Act, and will need to update their privacy policies and Web sites in order to do so. They also will need to implement a means of expeditiously providing the disclosures required by the law.

How will the Act be enforced?

The Act can be enforced by the California Attorney General, subject to a thirty-day cure period. The civil penalty for intentional violations of the Act is up to $7,500 per violation.

The Act also provides a private right of action that allows consumers to seek, either individually or as a class, statutory or actual damages and injunctive and other relief, if their sensitive personal information (more narrowly defined than under the rest of the Act) is subject to unauthorized access and exfiltration, theft or disclosure as a result of a business's failure to implement and maintain required reasonable security procedures. Statutory damages can be between $100 and $750 per California resident per incident, or actual damages, whichever is greater. However, it is not obvious what "per incident" means in this context, so the ceiling for statutory damages currently is unclear.

A consumer who wishes to bring an action under the Act will need to jump through a few hoops before he or she can proceed with a claim. A consumer seeking statutory damages must provide the defendant business with thirty days' notice of his or her intent to sue before filing an action. (Consumers seeking actual damages do not need to supply such notice.) If the business provides the consumer with an "express written statement" demonstrating that the violation has been cured, and that no further violation will occur, within thirty (30) days of receiving the consumer's notice, then the consumer cannot proceed with his or her action for statutory damages. A consumer who files an action must provide notice to the Attorney General within 30 days after filing. The Attorney General may (1) respond by notifying the consumer that the Attorney General will prosecute the action instead, (2) respond by notifying the consumer that he or she must not proceed with the action, or (3) not respond at all within 30 days, thereby allowing the consumer to proceed with their action.

When will the Act become effective?

The Act will take effect on January 1, 2020.

How similar is the Act to the EU's GDPR?

Although they do share some general features both the Act and the GDPR apply to companies located outside their borders, emphasize some of the same broad themes (such as the importance of access, transparency and accountability), and – perhaps most importantly – will require companies to expend a great deal of effort and resources to achieve compliance. However, that's really where the similarities end, as the laws' actual provisions overlap but are also quite different due to the GDPR's approach as being privacy by default and by design. This is fundamental to the GDPR's opt-in approach as opposed to the CCPA's far less stringent opt-out approach.

Perhaps the most basic difference is the fact that the GDPR is an omnibus law, while the Act is not. Not only does the GDPR regulate what disclosures companies must make to data subjects, it also covers procedures for data breach notification to individuals and regulators, data security implementation, cross-border data transfers and more. The Act is more limited, as there are existing Californian laws covering breaches and the like so it primarily is concerned with consumer privacy rights and disclosures made to consumers.

Both the GDPR and the Act give consumers certain rights as to their personal data, but those rights differ somewhat. While both the GDPR and the Act grant users the right to know what personal information a company has about them, Articles 15 and 20 of the GDPR impose additional requirements as to which data must be shared with the user, and the manner in which the disclosure must be made. Further, the GDPR offers a variety of additional rights to data subjects, including the right to be forgotten, the right to rectification, and the right to not be subject to a decision based solely on automated processing – none of which appear in the Act.

Nonetheless, the fact that the Act is less comprehensive than the GDPR the Act's sweeping scope should not be underestimated, and will require companies to expend a great deal of effort to achieve compliance.

It also is important to note that the GDPR does not subsume the Act, and that compliance with the GDPR does not ensure compliance with the Act. Most significantly, the two laws offer different – and potentially conflicting – approaches to consumer consent. The GDPR forbids companies from collecting, processing, or transferring personal information without a legal basis, and recognizes that user's informed and unambiguous consent may provide that legal basis. However, "opt out" mechanisms, such as pre-ticked check boxes, are not viewed as a means of obtaining valid consent under the GDPR. Instead, users must "opt in" to give their consent, such as by clicking on an unchecked box marked "I Agree" to indicate that they assent to the collection and use of their personal data. Unlike the GDPR, the Act does not require companies to obtain user consent to their processing of consumers' personal information. Instead, it requires business to offer consumers the opportunity to "opt out" of one specific use of their data: the sale of their personal information (except for minors under the age of 16, for whom consent must be given affirmatively). In short, the GDPR precludes the use of an "opt out" as a means of determining what may be done with users' personal information, while the Act requires the use of an "opt out" to prevent the sale of user data.

This marked difference between the GDPR and the Act presents a potential quandary for companies subject to both laws. Specifically, a company that sells its customers' personal data to third parties potentially may have to implement both opt-in and opt-out mechanisms in order to legally sell that data. If the company relies on user consent in order to sell or otherwise transfer the personal information of their EU customers to third parties, the company will have to implement the appropriate opt-in mechanisms for its customers in the EU. However, that same company will have to implement an opt-out mechanism to allow their California customers to prevent the sale of their personal information. Navigating compliance is likely to prove tricky for companies in this position. They may choose to find a legal basis other than consent in order to process EU user data, they may direct EU users to a Web site with an opt-in option and California (or more likely U.S.) users to a site with an opt-out function, or they may find another solution. Regardless, companies in this position will need to give some thought to their compliance strategies.

What is the potential impact of the Act?

As a practical matter, this law has the potential to change the privacy law landscape in the U.S. – not just California. As described above, the law's protection of California-based "consumers" means that many companies, even those based outside California and even outside the U.S., will be subject to its requirements. Businesses will incur significant compliance costs in order to update procedures, policies and Web sites in accordance with the new law. Additionally, the Act's grant of a private right of action means that companies will have to anticipate a possible flood of consumer-driven litigation.

We expect that the state legislature will continue to refine and amend the Act's privacy-related requirements before the final version of the law goes into effect on January 1, 2020.

One of the reasons that the CCPA was passed unanimously was due to the fact that a clean-up bill would be required. A clean-up bill is a special type of bill under the California legislative process whereby the bill is used to clean-up changes to a law following enactment of a prior bill that needs to be modified. Hence, the SB 1121 bill was introduced in the house of senate by the California Legislature to make technical corrections to the California Consumer Privacy Act, which was then known as AB 375 and signed into law on June 28, 2018.

The need for SB 1121 arose out of the abbreviated legislative process AB 375 had undergone on its journey into law. The deal on the legislation had to be done before the deadline to withdraw the November initiative from the ballot – so it was struck and passed very quickly. Despite the fast trip through the legislature, no one voted against it and it was signed into law by California Governor Jerry Brown a few hours before the deadline. However such a fast track approach had left the bill strewn with typos, nuances, ambiguities and apparent contradictions. The SB 1211 bill would be the vehicle used to manage all of these technical corrections to the CCPA.

However, despite its purpose as being a clean-up bill not all of the current amendments are entirely technical. One of the proposed changes created exclusion for political speech and journalism from the obligations imposed on businesses and the rights afforded to consumers as that was necessary to prevent potential conflict with the First Amendment. The changes further make clear that the private right of civil action only applies to breach violations, not the violation of individual provisions under the Act, where amongst other things there has been insufficient security controls or procedures in place that could have reasonably prevented the breach.

Now that the clean-up process is under way, organizations on both sides of the privacy divide have suggested substantive changes to the bill. The precise contours of the suggested changes became clearer as both a group of nearly 40 business organizations and the Electronic Frontier Foundation (EFF) have suggested changes to its terms. But it doesn't appear that these organizations are going to get additional input into the law's major provisions in 2018 according to the latest out of Senator Bill Dodd's office. Senator Dodd's spokesperson told the Sacramento Bee that there would be "no substantial changes" in SB 1121. Instead, any significant changes through the legislative process would be considered for 2019. On Sept 23rd SB 1121 was approved by the Governor and filed with the Secretary of State.

The text of the bill contained within "SB 1121, Dodd. California Consumer Privacy Act of 2018" as approved on Sept 23 makes only a handful of amendments to the CCPA.

1798.100 - Consumers right to receive information on privacy practices and access information

(a) A consumer shall have the right to request that a business that collects a consumer's personal information disclose to that consumer the categories and specific pieces of personal information the business have collected.

(b) A business that collects a consumer's personal information shall, at or before the point of collection, inform consumers as to the categories of personal information to be collected and the purposes for which the categories of personal information shall be used. A business shall not collect additional categories of personal information or use personal information collected for additional purposes without providing the consumer with notice consistent with this section.

(c) A business shall provide the information specified in subdivision (a) to a consumer only upon receipt of a verifiable consumer request.

(d) A business that receives a verifiable consumer request from a consumer to access personal information shall promptly take steps to disclose and deliver, free of charge to the consumer, the personal information required by this section. The information may be delivered by mail or electronically, and if provided electronically, the information shall be in a portable and, to the extent technically feasible, in a readily useable format that allows the consumer to transmit this information to another entity without hindrance. A business may provide personal information to a consumer at any time, but shall not be required to provide personal information to a consumer more than twice in a 12-month period.

(e) This section shall not require a business to retain any personal information collected for a single, one-time transaction, if such information is not sold or retained by the business or to reidentify or otherwise link information that is not maintained in a manner that would be considered personal information.

1798.105 - Consumers right to deletion

(a) A consumer shall have the right to request that a business delete any personal information about the consumer which the business has collected from the consumer.

(b) A business that collects personal information about consumers shall disclose, pursuant to Section 1798.130, the consumer's rights to request the deletion of the consumer's personal information.

(c) A business that receives a verifiable consumer request from a consumer to delete the consumer's personal information pursuant to subdivision (a) of this section shall delete the consumer's personal information from its records and direct any service providers to delete the consumer's personal information from their records.

(d) A business or a service provider shall not be required to comply with a consumer's request to delete the consumer's personal information if it is necessary for the business or service provider to maintain the consumer's personal information in order to:

(1) Complete the transaction for which the personal information was collected, provide a good or service requested by the

consumer, or reasonably anticipated within the context of a business's on-going business relationship with the consumer, or otherwise perform a contract between the business and the consumer.

(2) Detect security incidents, protect against malicious, deceptive, fraudulent, or illegal activity; or prosecute those responsible for that activity.

(3) Debug to identify and repair errors that impair existing intended functionality.

(4) Exercise free speech, ensure the right of another consumer to exercise his or her right of free speech, or exercise another right provided for by law.

(5) Comply with the California Electronic Communications Privacy Act pursuant to Chapter 3.6 (commencing with Section 1546) of Title 12 of Part 2 of the Penal Code.

(6) Engage in public or peer-reviewed scientific, historical, or statistical research in the public interest that adheres to all other applicable ethics and privacy laws, when the businesses' deletion of the information is likely to render impossible or seriously impair the achievement of such research, if the consumer has provided informed consent.

(7) To enable solely internal uses that are reasonably aligned with the expectations of the consumer based on the consumer's relationship with the business.

(8) Comply with a legal obligation.

(9) Otherwise use the consumer's personal information, internally, in a lawful manner that is compatible with the context in which the consumer provided the information.

1798.110 - Information required to be provided as part of an access request

(a) A consumer shall have the right to request that a business that collects personal information about the consumer disclose to the consumer the following:

(1) The categories of personal information it has collected about that consumer.

(2) The categories of sources from which the personal information is collected.

(3) The business or commercial purpose for collecting or selling personal information.

(4) The categories of third parties with whom the business shares personal information.

(5) The specific pieces of personal information it has collected about that consumer.

(b) A business that collects personal information about a consumer shall disclose to the consumer, pursuant to paragraph (3) of subdivision (a) of Section 1798.130, the information specified in subdivision (a) upon receipt of a verifiable request from the consumer.

(c) A business that collects personal information about consumers shall disclose, pursuant to subparagraph (B) of paragraph (5) of subdivision (a) of Section 1798.130:

(1) The categories of personal information it has collected about that consumer.

(2) The categories of sources from which the personal information is collected.

(3) The business or commercial purpose for collecting or selling personal information.

(4) The categories of third parties with whom the business shares personal information.

(5) The specific pieces of personal information the business has collected about that consumer.

(d) This section does not require a business to do the following:

(1) Retain any personal information about a consumer collected for a single one-time transaction if, in the ordinary course of business, that information about the consumer is not retained.

(2) Reidentify or otherwise link any data that, in the ordinary course of business, is not maintained in a manner that would be considered personal information.

1798.115 - Consumers right to receive information about onward disclosures

(a) A consumer shall have the right to request that a business that sells the consumer's personal information, or that discloses it for a business purpose, disclose to that consumer:

(1) The categories of personal information that the business collected about the consumer.

(2) The categories of personal information that the business sold about the consumer and the categories of third parties to whom the personal information was sold, by category or categories of personal information for each third party to whom the personal information was sold.

(3) The categories of personal information that the business disclosed about the consumer for a business purpose.

(b) A business that sells personal information about a consumer, or that discloses a consumer's personal information for a business purpose, shall disclose, pursuant to paragraph (4) of subdivision (a) of Section 1798.130, the information specified in subdivision (a) to the consumer upon receipt of a verifiable consumer request from the consumer.

(c) A business that sells consumers' personal information, or that discloses consumers' personal information for a business purpose, shall disclose, pursuant to subparagraph (C) of paragraph (5) of subdivision (a) of Section 1798.130:

(1) The category or categories of consumers' personal information it has sold, or if the business has not sold consumers' personal information, it shall disclose that fact.

(2) The category or categories of consumers' personal information it has disclosed for a business purpose, or if the business has not disclosed the consumers' personal information for a business purpose, it shall disclose that fact.

(d) A third party shall not sell personal information about a consumer that has been sold to the third party by a business unless the consumer has received explicit notice and is provided an opportunity to exercise the right to opt out pursuant to Section 1798.120.

1798.120 - Consumer right to prohibit the sale of their information

(a) A consumer shall have the right, at any time, to direct a business that sells personal information about the consumer to third parties not to sell the consumer's personal information. This right may be referred to as the right to opt out.

(b) A business that sells consumers' personal information to third parties shall provide notice to consumers, pursuant to subdivision (a) of Section 1798.135, that this information may be sold and that consumers have the right to opt out of the sale of their personal information.

(c) Notwithstanding subdivision (a), a business shall not sell the personal information of consumers if the business has actual knowledge that the consumer is less than 16 years of age, unless the consumer, in the case of consumers between 13 and 16 years of age, or the consumer's parent or guardian, in the case of consumers who are less than 13 years of age, has affirmatively authorized the sale of the consumer's personal information. A business that willfully disregards the consumer's age shall be deemed to have had actual knowledge of the consumer's age. This right may be referred to as the "right to opt in."

(d) A business that has received direction from a consumer not to sell the consumer's personal information or, in the case of a minor consumer's personal information has not received consent to sell the minor consumer's personal information shall be prohibited, pursuant to paragraph (4) of subdivision (a) of Section 1798.135, from selling the consumer's personal information after its receipt of the consumer's direction, unless the consumer subsequently provides express authorization for the sale of the consumer's personal information.

1798.125 - Price discrimination based upon the exercise of the opt-out right

(a)

(1) A business shall not discriminate against a consumer because the consumer exercised any of the consumer's rights under this title, including, but not limited to, by:

(A) Denying goods or services to the consumer.

(B) Charging different prices or rates for goods or services, including through the use of discounts or other benefits or imposing penalties.

(C) Providing a different level or quality of goods or services to the consumer.

(D) Suggesting that the consumer will receive a different price or rate for goods or services or a different level or quality of goods or services.

(2) Nothing in this subdivision prohibits a business from charging a consumer a different price or rate, or from providing a different level or quality of goods or services to the consumer, if that

difference is reasonably related to the value provided to the consumer by the consumer's data.

(b)

(1) A business may offer financial incentives, including payments to consumers as compensation, for the collection of personal information, the sale of personal information, or the deletion of personal information. A business may also offer a different price, rate, level, or quality of goods or services to the consumer if that price or difference is directly related to the value provided to the consumer by the consumer's data.

(2) A business that offers any financial incentives pursuant to subdivision (a), shall notify consumers of the financial incentives pursuant to Section 1798.135.

(3) A business may enter a consumer into a financial incentive program only if the consumer gives the business prior opt-in consent pursuant to Section 1798.135 which clearly describes the material terms of the financial incentive program, and which may be revoked by the consumer at any time.

(4) A business shall not use financial incentive practices that are unjust, unreasonable, coercive, or usurious in nature.

1798.130 - Means for exercising consumer rights

(a) In order to comply with Sections 1798.100, 1798.105, 1798.110, 1798.115, and 1798.125, a business shall in a form that is reasonably accessible to consumers:

(1) Make available to consumers two or more designated methods for submitting requests for information required to be disclosed

pursuant to Sections 1798.110 and 1798.115, including, at a minimum, a toll-free telephone number, and if the business maintains an Internet Web site, a Web site address.

(2) Disclose and deliver the required information to a consumer free of charge within 45 days of receiving a verifiable consumer request from the consumer. The business shall promptly take steps to determine whether the request is a verifiable consumer request, but this shall not extend the business's duty to disclose and deliver the information within 45 days of receipt of the consumer's request. The time period to provide the required information may be extended once by an additional 45 days when reasonably necessary, provided the consumer is provided notice of the extension within the first 45-day period. The disclosure shall cover the 12-month period preceding the business's receipt of the verifiable consumer request and shall be made in writing and delivered through the consumer's account with the business, if the consumer maintains an account with the business, or by mail or electronically at the consumer's option if the consumer does not maintain an account with the business, in a readily useable format that allows the consumer to transmit this information from one entity to another entity without hindrance. The business shall not require the consumer to create an account with the business in order to make a verifiable consumer request.

(3) For purposes of subdivision (b) of Section 1798.110:

(A) To identify the consumer, associate the information provided by the consumer in the verifiable consumer request to any personal information previously collected by the business about the consumer.

~ 110 ~

(B) Identify by category or categories the personal information collected about the consumer in the preceding 12 months by reference to the enumerated category or categories in subdivision (c) that most closely describes the personal information collected.

(4) For purposes of subdivision (b) of Section 1798.115:

(A) Identify the consumer and associate the information provided by the consumer in the verifiable consumer request to any personal information previously collected by the business about the consumer.

(B) Identify by category or categories the personal information of the consumer that the business sold in the preceding 12 months by reference to the enumerated category in subdivision (c) that most closely describes the personal information, and provide the categories of third parties to whom the consumer's personal information was sold in the preceding 12 months by reference to the enumerated category or categories in subdivision (c) that most closely describes the personal information sold. The business shall disclose the information in a list that is separate from a list generated for the purposes of subparagraph (C).

(C) Identify by category or categories the personal information of the consumer that the business disclosed for a business purpose in the preceding 12 months by reference to the enumerated category or categories in subdivision (c) that most closely describes the personal information, and provide the categories of third parties to whom the consumer's personal information was disclosed for a business purpose in the preceding 12 months by reference to the enumerated category or categories in subdivision (c) that most closely describes the personal information disclosed. The business shall disclose the information in a list that is separate from a list generated for the purposes of subparagraph (B).

(5) Disclose the following information in its online privacy policy or policies if the business has an online privacy policy or policies and in any California-specific description of consumers' privacy rights, or if the business does not maintain those policies, on its Internet Web site, and update that information at least once every 12 months:

(A) A description of a consumer's rights pursuant to Sections 1798.110, 1798.115, and 1798.125 and one or more designated methods for submitting requests.

(B) For purposes of subdivision (c) of Section 1798.110, a list of the categories of personal information it has collected about consumers in the preceding 12 months by reference to the enumerated category or categories in subdivision (c) that most closely describe the personal information collected.

(C) For purposes of paragraphs (1) and (2) of subdivision (c) of Section 1798.115, two separate lists:

(i) A list of the categories of personal information it has sold about consumers in the preceding 12 months by reference to the enumerated category or categories in subdivision (c) that most closely describe the personal information sold, or if the business has not sold consumers' personal information in the preceding 12 months, the business shall disclose that fact.

(ii) A list of the categories of personal information it has disclosed about consumers for a business purpose in the preceding 12 months by reference to the enumerated category in subdivision (c) that most closely describe the personal information disclosed, or if the business has not disclosed consumers' personal information for a business purpose in the preceding 12 months, the business shall disclose that fact.

(6) Ensure that all individuals responsible for handling consumer inquiries about the business's privacy practices or the business's compliance with this title are informed of all requirements in Sections 1798.110, 1798.115, 1798.125, and this section, and how to direct consumers to exercise their rights under those sections.

(7) Use any personal information collected from the consumer in connection with the business's verification of the consumer's request solely for the purposes of verification.

(b) A business is not obligated to provide the information required by Sections 1798.110 and 1798.115 to the same consumer more than twice in a 12-month period.

(c) The categories of personal information required to be disclosed pursuant to Sections 1798.110 and 1798.115 shall follow the definition of personal information in Section 1798.140.

1798.135 – Opt out link

(a) A business that is required to comply with Section 1798.120 shall, in a form that is reasonably accessible to consumers:

(1) Provide a clear and conspicuous link on the business's Internet homepage, titled "Do Not Sell My Personal Information," to an Internet Web page that enables a consumer, or a person authorized by the consumer, to opt out of the sale of the consumer's personal information. A business shall not require a consumer to create an account in order to direct the business not to sell the consumer's personal information.

(2) Include a description of a consumer's rights pursuant to Section 1798.120, along with a separate link to the "Do Not Sell My Personal Information" Internet Web page in:

(A)   Its online privacy policy or policies if the business has an online privacy policy or policies.

(B) Any California-specific description of consumers' privacy rights.

(3) Ensure that all individuals responsible for handling consumer inquiries about the business's privacy practices or the business's compliance with this title are informed of all requirements in Section 1798.120 and this section and how to direct consumers to exercise their rights under those sections.

(4) For consumers who exercise their right to opt out of the sale of their personal information, refrain from selling personal information collected by the business about the consumer.

(5) For a consumer who has opted-out of the sale of the consumer's personal information, respect the consumer's decision

to opt-out for at least 12 months before requesting that the consumer authorize the sale of the consumer's personal information.

(6) Use any personal information collected from the consumer in connection with the submission of the consumer's opt-out request solely for the purposes of complying with the opt-out request.

(b) Nothing in this title shall be construed to require a business to comply with the title by including the required links and text on the homepage that the business makes available to the public generally, if the business maintains a separate and additional homepage that is dedicated to California consumers and that includes the required links and text, and the business takes reasonable steps to ensure that California consumers are directed to the homepage for California consumers and not the homepage made available to the public generally.

(c) A consumer may authorize another person solely to opt-out of the sale of the consumer's personal information on the consumer's behalf, and a business shall comply with an opt-out request received from a person authorized by the consumer to act on the consumer's behalf, pursuant to regulations adopted by the Attorney General.

1798.140 - Definitions

For purposes of this title:

(a) "Aggregate consumer information" means information that relates to a group or category of consumers, from which individual consumer identities have been removed, that is not linked or reasonably linkable to any consumer or household, including via a device. "Aggregate consumer information" does not mean one or more individual consumer records that have been deidentified.

(b) "Biometric information" means an individual's physiological, biological or behavioural characteristics, including an individual's deoxyribonucleic acid (DNA) that can be used, singly or in combination with each other or with other identifying data, to establish individual identity. Biometric information includes, but is not limited to, imagery of the iris, retina, fingerprint, face, hand, palm, vein patterns, and voice recordings, from which an identifier template, such as a faceprint, a minutiae template, or a voiceprint, can be extracted, and keystroke patterns or rhythms, gait patterns or rhythms, and sleep, health, or exercise data that contain identifying information.

(c) "Business" means:

(1) A sole proprietorship, partnership, limited liability company, corporation, association, or other legal entity that is organized or operated for the profit or financial benefit of its shareholders or other owners, that collects consumers' personal information, or on the behalf of which such information is collected and that alone, or jointly with others, determines the purposes and means of the processing of consumers' personal information, that does business in the State of California, and that satisfies one or more of the following thresholds:

(A) Has annual gross revenues in excess of twenty-five million dollars ($25,000,000), as adjusted pursuant to paragraph (5) of subdivision (a) of Section 1798.185

(B) Alone or in combination, annually buys, receives for the business' commercial purposes, sells, or shares for commercial purposes, alone or in combination, the personal information of 50,000 or more consumers, households, or devices.

(C) Derives 50 percent or more of its annual revenues from selling consumers' personal information.

(2) Any entity that controls or is controlled by a business, as defined in paragraph (1), and that shares common branding with the business. "Control" or "controlled" means ownership of, or the power to vote, more than 50 percent of the outstanding shares of any class of voting security of a business; control in any manner over the election of a majority of the directors, or of individuals exercising similar functions; or the power to exercise a controlling influence over the management of a company. "Common branding" means a shared name, servicemark, or trademark.

(d) "Business purpose" means the use of personal information for the business' or a service provider's operational purposes, or other notified purposes, provided that the use of personal information shall be reasonably necessary and proportionate to achieve the operational purpose for which the personal information was collected or processed or for another operational purpose that is compatible with the context in which the personal information was collected. Business purposes are:

(1) Auditing related to a current interaction with the consumer and concurrent transactions, including, but not limited to, counting ad impressions to unique visitors, verifying positioning and quality of

ad impressions, and auditing compliance with this specification and other standards.

(2) Detecting security incidents, protecting against malicious, deceptive, fraudulent, or illegal activity, and prosecuting those responsible for that activity.

(3) Debugging to identify and repair errors that impair existing intended functionality.

(4) Short-term, transient use, provided the personal information that is not disclosed to another third party and is not used to build a profile about a consumer or otherwise alter an individual consumer's experience outside the current interaction, including, but not limited to, the contextual customization of ads shown as part of the same interaction.

(5) Performing services on behalf of the business or service provider, including maintaining or servicing accounts, providing customer service, processing or fulfilling orders and transactions, verifying customer information, processing payments, providing financing, providing advertising or marketing services, providing analytic services, or providing similar services on behalf of the business or service provider.

(6) Undertaking internal research for technological development and demonstration.

(7) Undertaking activities to verify or maintain the quality or safety of a service or device that is owned, manufactured, manufactured for, or controlled by the business, and to improve,

upgrade, or enhance the service or device that is owned, manufactured, manufactured for, or controlled by the business.

(e) "Collects," "collected," or "collection" means buying, renting, gathering, obtaining, receiving, or accessing any personal information pertaining to a consumer by any means. This includes receiving information from the consumer, either actively or passively, or by observing the consumer's behaviour.

(f) "Commercial purposes" means to advance a person's commercial or economic interests, such as by inducing another person to buy, rent, lease, join, subscribe to, provide, or exchange products, goods, property, information, or services, or enabling or effecting, directly or indirectly, a commercial transaction. "Commercial purposes" do not include for the purpose of engaging in speech that state or federal courts have recognized as non-commercial speech, including political speech and journalism.

(g) "Consumer" means a natural person who is a California resident, as defined in Section 17014 of Title 18 of the California Code of Regulations, as that section read on September 1, 2017, however identified, including by any unique identifier.

(h) "Deidentified" means information that cannot reasonably identify, relate to, describe, be capable of being associated with, or be linked, directly or indirectly, to a particular consumer, provided that a business that uses deidentified information:

(1) Has implemented technical safeguards that prohibit re-identification of the consumer to whom the information may pertain.

(2) Has implemented business processes that specifically prohibit re-identification of the information.

(3) Has implemented business processes to prevent inadvertent release of deidentified information.

(4) Makes no attempt to reidentify the information.

(i) "Designated methods for submitting requests" means a mailing address, email address, Internet Web page, Internet Web portal, toll-free telephone number, or other applicable contact information, whereby consumers may submit a request or direction under this title, and any new, consumer-friendly means of contacting a business, as approved by the Attorney General pursuant to Section 1798.185.

(j) "Device" means any physical object that is capable of connecting to the Internet, directly or indirectly, or to another device.

(k) "Health insurance information" means a consumer's insurance policy number or subscriber identification number, any unique identifier used by a health insurer to identify the consumer, or any information in the consumer's application and claims history, including any appeals records, if the information is linked or reasonably linkable to a consumer or household, including via a device, by a business or service provider.

(l) "Homepage" means the introductory page of an Internet Web site and any Internet Web page where personal information is collected. In the case of an online service, such as a mobile application, homepage means the application's platform page or download page, a link within the application, such as from the application configuration, "About," "Information," or settings page, and any other location that allows consumers to review the notice required by subdivision (a) of Section 1798.145, including, but not limited to, before downloading the application.

(m) "Infer" or "inference" means the derivation of information, data, assumptions, or conclusions from facts, evidence, or another source of information or data.

(n) "Person" means an individual, proprietorship, firm, partnership, joint venture, syndicate, business trust, company, corporation, limited liability company, association, committee, and any other organization or group of persons acting in concert.

(o)

(1) "Personal information" means information that identifies, relates to, describes, is capable of being associated with, or could reasonably be linked, directly or indirectly, with a particular consumer or household. Personal information includes, but is not limited to, the following if it identifies, relates to, describes, is capable of being associated with, or could be reasonably linked, directly or indirectly, with a particular consumer or household:

(A) Identifiers such as a real name, alias, postal address, unique personal identifier, online identifier Internet Protocol address, email address, account name, social security number, driver's license number, passport number, or other similar identifiers.

(B) Any categories of personal information described in subdivision (e) of Section 1798.80.

(C) Characteristics of protected classifications under California or federal law.

(D) Commercial information, including records of personal property, products or services purchased, obtained, or considered, or other purchasing or consuming histories or tendencies.

(E) Biometric information.

(F) Internet or other electronic network activity information, including, but not limited to, browsing history, search history, and information regarding a consumer's interaction with an Internet Web site, application, or advertisement.

(G) Geolocation data.

(H) Audio, electronic, visual, thermal, olfactory, or similar information.

(I) Professional or employment-related information

(J) Education information, defined as information that is not publicly available personally identifiable information as defined in the Family Educational Rights and Privacy Act (20 U.S.C. section 1232g, 34 C.F.R. Part 99).

(K) Inferences drawn from any of the information identified in this subdivision to create a profile about a consumer reflecting the consumer's preferences, characteristics, psychological trends, predispositions, behaviour, attitudes, intelligence, abilities, and aptitudes.

(2) "Personal information" does not include publicly available information. For these purposes, "publicly available" means

information that is lawfully made available from federal, state, or local government records, if any conditions associated with such information. "Publicly available" does not mean biometric information collected by a business about a consumer without the consumer's knowledge. Information is not "publicly available" if that data is used for a purpose that is not compatible with the purpose for which the data is maintained and made available in the government records or for which it is publicly maintained. "Publicly available" does not include consumer information that is deidentified or aggregate consumer information.

(p) "Probabilistic identifier" means the identification of a consumer or a device to a degree of certainty of more probable than not based on any categories of personal information included in, or similar to, the categories enumerated in the definition of personal information.

(q) "Processing" means any operation or set of operations that are performed on personal data or on sets of personal data, whether or not by automated means.

(r) "Pseudonymize" or "Pseudonymization" means the processing of personal information in a manner that renders the personal information no longer attributable to a specific consumer without the use of additional information, provided that the additional information is kept separately and is subject to technical and organizational measures to ensure that the personal information is not attributed to an identified or identifiable consumer.

(s) "Research" means scientific, systematic study and observation, including basic research or applied research that is in the public interest and that adheres to all other applicable ethics and privacy laws or studies conducted in the public interest in the area of public health.

Research with personal information that may have been collected from a consumer in the course of the consumer's interactions with a business's service or device for other purposes shall be:

(1) Compatible with the business purpose for which the personal information was collected.

(2) Subsequently pseudonymized and deidentified, or deidentified and in the aggregate, such that the information cannot reasonably identify, relate to, describe, be capable of being associated with, or be linked, directly or indirectly, to a particular consumer.

(3) Made subject to technical safeguards that prohibit re-identification of the consumer to whom the information may pertain.

(4) Subject to business processes that specifically prohibit re-identification of the information.

(5) Made subject to business processes to prevent inadvertent release of deidentified information.

(6) Protected from any re-identification attempts.

(7) Used solely for research purposes that is compatible with the context in which the personal information was collected.

(8) Not be used for any commercial purpose.

(9) Subjected by the business conducting the research to additional security controls limit access to the research data to only those individuals in a business as are necessary to carry out the research purpose.

(t)

(1) "Sell," "selling," "sale," or "sold," means selling, renting, releasing, disclosing, disseminating, making available, transferring, or otherwise communicating orally, in writing, or by electronic or other means, a consumer's personal information by the business to another business or a third party for monetary or other valuable consideration.

(2) For purposes of this title, a business does not sell personal information when:

(A) A consumer uses or directs the business to intentionally disclose personal information or uses the business to intentionally interact with a third party, provided the third party does not also sell the personal information, unless that disclosure would be consistent with the provisions of this title. An intentional interaction occurs when the consumer intends to interact with the third party, via one or more deliberate interactions. Hovering over, muting, pausing, or closing a given piece of content does not constitute a consumer's intent to interact with a third party.

(B) The business uses or shares an identifier for a consumer who has opted out of the sale of the consumer's personal information for the purposes of alerting third parties that the consumer has opted out of the sale of the consumer's personal information.

(C) The business uses or shares with a service provider personal information of a consumer that is necessary to perform a business purpose if both of the following conditions are met:

(i) The business has provided notice that information being used or shared in its terms and conditions consistent with Section 1798.135.

(ii) The service provider does not further collect, sell, or use the personal information of the consumer except as necessary to perform the business purpose.

(D) The business transfers to a third party the personal information of a consumer as an asset that is part of a merger, acquisition, bankruptcy, or other transaction in which the third party assumes control of all or part of the business provided that information is used or shared consistently with Sections 1798.110 and 1798.115. If a third party materially alters how it uses or shares the personal information of a consumer in a manner that is materially inconsistent with the promises made at the time of collection, it shall provide prior notice of the new or changed practice to the consumer. The notice shall be sufficiently prominent and robust to ensure that existing consumers can easily exercise their choices consistently with Section 1798.120. This subparagraph does not authorize a business to make material, retroactive privacy policy changes or make other changes in their privacy policy in a manner that would violate the Unfair and Deceptive Practices Act (Chapter 5 (commencing with Section

17200) of Part 2 of Division 7 of the Business and Professions Code).

(u) "Service" or "services" means work, labour, and services, including services furnished in connection with the sale or repair of goods.

(v) "Service provider" means a sole proprietorship, partnership, limited liability company, corporation, association, or other legal entity that is organized or operated for the profit or financial benefit of its shareholders or other owners, that processes information on behalf of a business and to which the business discloses a consumer's personal information for a business purpose pursuant to a written contract, provided that the contract prohibits the entity receiving the information from retaining, using, or disclosing the personal information for any purpose other than for the specific purpose of performing the services specified in the contract for the business, or as otherwise permitted by this title, including retaining, using, or disclosing the personal information for a commercial purpose other than providing the services specified in the contract with the business.

(w) "Third party" means a person who is not any of the following:

(1) The business that collects personal information from consumers under this title.

(2)

(A) A person to whom the business discloses a consumer's personal information for a business purpose pursuant to a written contract, provided that the contract:

(i) Prohibits the person receiving the personal information from:

(I) Selling the personal information

(II) Retaining, using, or disclosing the personal information for any purpose other than for the specific purpose of performing the services specified in the contract, including retaining, using, or disclosing the personal information for a commercial purpose other than providing the services specified in the contract

(III) Retaining, using, or disclosing the information outside of the direct business relationship between the person and the business.

(B) Includes a certification made by the person receiving the personal information that the person understands the restrictions in subparagraph (A) and will comply with them.

(3) A person covered by this paragraph that violates any of the restrictions set forth in this title shall be liable for the violations. A business that discloses personal information to a person covered by this paragraph in compliance with this paragraph shall not be liable under this title if the person receiving the personal information uses it in violation of the restrictions set forth in this title, provided that, at the time of disclosing the personal information, the business does not have actual knowledge, or reason to believe, that the person intends to commit such a violation.

(x) "Unique identifier" or "Unique personal identifier" means a persistent identifier that can be used to recognize a consumer, a family, or a device that is linked to a consumer or family, over time and across different services, including, but not limited to, a device identifier; an Internet Protocol address; cookies, beacons, pixel tags, mobile ad identifiers, or similar technology; customer number, unique pseudonym, or user alias; telephone numbers, or other forms of persistent or probabilistic identifiers that can be used to identify a particular consumer or device. For purposes of this subdivision, "family" means a custodial parent or guardian and any minor children over which the parent or guardian has custody.

(y) "Verifiable consumer request" means a request that is made by a consumer, by a consumer on behalf of the consumer's minor child, or by a natural person or a person registered with the Secretary of State, authorized by the consumer to act on the consumer's behalf, and that the business can reasonably verify, pursuant to regulations adopted by the Attorney General pursuant to paragraph (7) of subdivision (a) of Section 1798.185 to be the consumer about whom the business has collected personal information. A business is not obligated to provide information to the consumer pursuant to Sections 1798.110 and 1798.115 if the business cannot verify, pursuant this subdivision and regulations adopted by the Attorney General pursuant to paragraph (7) of subdivision (a) of Section 1798.185, that the consumer making the request is the consumer about whom the business has collected information or is a person authorized by the consumer to act on such consumer's behalf.

1798.145 - Interaction with other statutes, rights, and obligations

(a) The obligations imposed on businesses by this title shall not restrict a business's ability to:

(1) Comply with federal, state, or local laws.

(2) Comply with a civil, criminal, or regulatory inquiry, investigation, subpoena, or summons by federal, state, or local authorities.

(3) Cooperate with law enforcement agencies concerning conduct or activity that the business, service provider, or third party reasonably and in good faith believes may violate federal, state, or local law.

(4) Exercise or defend legal claims.

(5) Collect, use, retain, sell, or disclose consumer information that is deidentified or in the aggregate consumer information.

(6) Collect or sell a consumer's personal information if every aspect of that commercial conduct takes place wholly outside of California. For purposes of this title, commercial conduct takes place wholly outside of California if the business collected that information while the consumer was outside of California, no part of the sale of the consumer's personal information occurred in California, and no personal information collected while the consumer was in California is sold. This paragraph shall not permit a business from storing, including on a device, personal information about a consumer when the consumer is in California and then collecting that personal information when the consumer and stored personal information is outside of California.

(b) The obligations imposed on businesses by Sections 1798.110 to 1798.135, inclusive, shall not apply where compliance by the business with the title would violate an evidentiary privilege under California law and shall not prevent a business from providing the personal information of a consumer to a person covered by an evidentiary privilege under California law as part of a privileged communication.

(c)

(1) This title shall not apply to any of the following:

(A) Medical information governed by the Confidentiality of Medical Information Act (Part 2.6 (commencing with Section 56) of Division 1) or protected health information that is collected by a covered entity or business associate governed by the privacy, security, and breach notification rules issued by the United States Department of Health and Human Services, Parts 160 and 164 of Title 45 of the Code of Federal Regulations, established pursuant to the Health Insurance Portability and Accountability Act of 1996 (Public Law 104-191) and the Health Information Technology for Economic and Clinical Health Act (Public Law 111-5)

(B) A provider of health care governed by the Confidentiality of Medical Information Act (Part 2.6 (commencing with Section 56) of Division 1) or a covered entity governed by the privacy, security, and breach notification rules issued by the United States Department of Health and Human Services, Parts 160 and 164 of Title 45 of the Code of Federal Regulations, established pursuant to the Health Insurance Portability and Accountability Act of 1996 (Public Law 104-191), to the extent the provider or covered entity maintains patient information in the same manner as medical information or protected health information as described in subparagraph (A) of this section.

(C) Information collected as part of a clinical trial subject to the Federal Policy for the Protection of Human Subjects, also known as the Common Rule, pursuant to good clinical practice guidelines issued by the International Council for Harmonisation or pursuant to human subject protection requirements of the United States Food and Drug Administration.

(2) For purposes of this subdivision, the definitions of "medical information" and "provider of health care" in Section 56.05 shall apply and the definitions of "business associate," "covered entity," and "protected health information" in Section 160.103 of Title 45 of the Code of Federal Regulations shall apply.

(d) This title shall not apply to the sale of personal information to or from a consumer reporting agency if that information is to be reported in, or used to generate, a consumer report as defined by subdivision (d) of Section 1681a of Title 15 of the United States Code, and use of that information is limited by the federal Fair Credit Reporting Act (15 U.S.C. Sec. 1681 et seq.).

(e) This title shall not apply to personal information collected, processed, sold, or disclosed pursuant to the federal Gramm-Leach-Bliley Act (Public Law 106-102), and implementing regulations, or the California Financial Information Privacy Act (Division 1.4 (commencing with Section 4050) of the Financial Code). This subdivision shall not apply to Section 1798.150.

(f) This title shall not apply to personal information collected, processed, sold, or disclosed pursuant to the Driver's Privacy Protection Act of 1994 (18 U.S.C. Sec. 2721 et seq.). This subdivision shall not apply to Section 1798.150.

(g) Notwithstanding a business's obligations to respond to and honour consumer rights requests pursuant to this title:

(1) A time period for a business to respond to any verified consumer request may be extended by up to 90 additional days where necessary, taking into account the complexity and number of the requests. The business shall inform the consumer of any such extension within 45 days of receipt of the request, together with the reasons for the delay.

(2) If the business does not take action on the request of the consumer, the business shall inform the consumer, without delay and at the latest within the time period permitted of response by this section, of the reasons for not taking action and any rights the consumer may have to appeal the decision to the business.

(3) If requests from a consumer are manifestly unfounded or excessive, in particular because of their repetitive character, a business may either charge a reasonable fee, taking into account the administrative costs of providing the information or communication or taking the action requested, or refuse to act on the request and notify the consumer of the reason for refusing the request. The business shall bear the burden of demonstrating that any verified consumer request is manifestly unfounded or excessive.

(h) A business that discloses personal information to a service provider shall not be liable under this title if the service provider receiving the personal information uses it in violation of the restrictions set forth in the title, provided that, at the time of disclosing the personal information, the business does not have actual knowledge, or reason to believe, that the service provider intends to commit such a violation. A service provider shall likewise not be liable under this title for the obligations of a business for which it provides services as set forth in this title.

(i) This title shall not be construed to require a business to reidentify or otherwise link information that is not maintained in a manner that would be considered personal information.

(j) The rights afforded to consumers and the obligations imposed on the business in this title shall not adversely affect the rights and freedoms of other consumers.

(k) The rights afforded to consumers and the obligations imposed on any business under this title shall not apply to the extent that they infringe on the non-commercial activities of a person or entity described in subdivision (b) of Section 2 of Article I of the California Constitution.

1798.150 - Civil Actions

(a)

(1) Any consumer whose non-encrypted or non-redacted personal information, as defined in subparagraph (A) of paragraph (1) of subdivision (d) of Section 1798.81.5, is subject to an unauthorized access and exfiltration, theft, or disclosure as a result of the business's violation of the duty to implement and maintain

reasonable security procedures and practices appropriate to the nature of the information to protect the personal information may institute a civil action for any of the following:

(A) To recover damages in an amount not less than one hundred dollars ($100) and not greater than seven hundred and fifty ($750) per consumer per incident or actual damages, whichever is greater.

(B) Injunctive or declaratory relief.

(C) Any other relief the court deems proper.

(2) In assessing the amount of statutory damages, the court shall consider any one or more of the relevant circumstances presented by any of the parties to the case, including, but not limited to, the nature and seriousness of the misconduct, the number of violations, the persistence of the misconduct, the length of time over which the misconduct occurred, the willfulness of the defendant's misconduct, and the defendant's assets, liabilities, and net worth.

(b) Actions pursuant to this section may be brought by a consumer if prior to initiating any action against a business for statutory damages on an individual or class-wide basis, a consumer provides a business 30 days' written notice identifying the specific provisions of this title the consumer alleges have been or are being violated. In the event a cure is possible, if within the 30 days the business actually cures the noticed violation and provides the consumer an express written statement that the violations have been cured and that no further violations shall occur, no action for individual statutory damages or class-wide statutory damages may be initiated against the business. No notice shall be required prior to an individual consumer initiating an action solely for actual pecuniary damages suffered as a result of the alleged violations of this title. If a business continues to violate this title in breach of the express written statement provided to the consumer under this section, the consumer may initiate an action against the business to enforce the written statement and may pursue statutory damages for each breach of the express written statement, as well as any other violation of the title that postdates the written statement.

(c) The cause of action established by this section shall apply only to violations as defined in subdivision (a) and shall not be based on violations of any other section of this title.

Nothing in this title shall be interpreted to serve as the basis for a private right of action under any other law. This shall not be construed to relieve any party from any duties or obligations imposed under other law or the United States or California Constitution.

1798.155 - Attorney General Guidance and enforcement

(a) Any business or third party may seek the opinion of the Attorney General for guidance on how to comply with the provisions of this title.

(b) A business shall be in violation of this title if it fails to cure any alleged violation within 30 days after being notified of alleged noncompliance. Any business, service provider, or other person that violates this title shall be subject to an injunction and liable for a civil penalty of not more than two thousand five hundred dollars ($2,500) for each violation or seven thousand five hundred dollars ($7,500) for each intentional violation, which shall be assessed and recovered in a civil action brought in the name of the people of the State of California by the Attorney General. The civil penalties provided for in this section shall be exclusively assessed and recovered in a civil action brought in the name of the people of the State of California by the Attorney General.

(c) Any civil penalty assessed for a violation of this title, and the proceeds of any settlement of an action brought pursuant to subdivision (b), shall be deposited in the Consumer Privacy Fund, created within the General Fund pursuant to subdivision (a) of Section 1798.160 with the intent to fully offset any costs incurred by the state courts and the Attorney General in connection with this title.

1798.160 – Consumer privacy fund

(a) A special fund to be known as the "Consumer Privacy Fund" is hereby created within the General Fund in the State Treasury, and is available upon appropriation by the Legislature to offset any costs incurred by the state courts in connection with actions brought to enforce this title and any costs incurred by the Attorney General in carrying out the Attorney General's duties under this title.

(b) Funds transferred to the Consumer Privacy Fund shall be used exclusively to offset any costs incurred by the state courts and the Attorney General in connection with this title. These funds shall not be subject to appropriation or transfer by the Legislature for any other purpose, unless the Director of Finance determines that the funds are in excess of the funding needed to fully offset the costs incurred by the state courts and the Attorney General in connection with this title, in which case the Legislature may appropriate excess funds for other purposes.

1798.175 - Intent, scope, and construction of title

This title is intended to further the constitutional right of privacy and to supplement existing laws relating to consumers' personal information, including, but not limited to, Chapter 22 (commencing with Section 22575) of Division 8 of the Business and Professions Code and Title 1.81 (commencing with Section 1798.80). The provisions of this title are not limited to information collected electronically or over the Internet, but apply to the collection and sale of all personal information collected by a business from consumers. Wherever possible, law relating to consumers' personal information should be construed to harmonize with the provisions of this title, but in the event of a conflict between other laws and the provisions of this title, the provisions of the law that afford the greatest protection for the right of privacy for consumers shall control.

1798.180 -Preemption

This title is a matter of state-wide concern and supersedes and pre-empts all rules, regulations, codes, ordinances, and other laws adopted by a city, county, city and county, municipality, or local agency regarding the collection and sale of consumers' personal information by a business.

1798.185 - Adoption of regulations

(a) On or before July 1, 2020, the Attorney General shall solicit broad public participation and adopt regulations to further the purposes of this title, including, but not limited to, the following areas:

(1) Updating as needed additional categories of personal information to those enumerated in subdivision (c) of Section 1798.130 and subdivision (o) of Section 1798.140 in order to address changes in technology, data collection practices, obstacles to implementation, and privacy concerns.

(2) Updating as needed the definition of unique identifiers to address changes in technology, data collection, obstacles to implementation, and privacy concerns, and additional categories to the definition of designated methods for submitting requests to facilitate a consumer's ability to obtain information from a business pursuant to Section 1798.130.

(3) Establishing any exceptions necessary to comply with state or federal law, including, but not limited to, those relating to trade secrets and intellectual property rights, within one year of passage of this title and as needed thereafter.

(4) Establishing rules and procedures for the following:

(A) To facilitate and govern the submission of a request by a consumer to opt out of the sale of personal information pursuant to paragraph (1) of subdivision (a) of Section 1798.145.

(B) To govern business compliance with a consumer's opt-out request.

(C) For the development and use of a recognizable and uniform opt-out logo or button by all businesses to promote consumer awareness of the opportunity to opt-out of the sale of personal information.

(5) Adjusting the monetary threshold in subparagraph (A) of paragraph (1) of subdivision (c) of Section 1798.140 in January of every odd-numbered year to reflect any increase in the Consumer Price Index.

(6) Establishing rules, procedures, and any exceptions necessary to ensure that the notices and information that businesses are required to provide pursuant to this title are provided in a manner that may be easily understood by the average consumer, are accessible to consumers with disabilities, and are available in the language primarily used to interact with the consumer, including establishing rules and guidelines regarding financial incentive offerings, within one year of passage of this title and as needed thereafter.

(7) Establishing rules and procedures to further the purposes of Sections 1798.110 and 1798.115 and to facilitate a consumer's or the consumer's authorized agent's ability to obtain information pursuant to Section 1798.130, with the goal of minimizing the administrative burden on consumers, taking into account available technology, security concerns, and the burden on the business, to govern a business' determination that a request for information received by a consumer is a verifiable consumer request, including treating a request submitted through a password-protected account maintained by the consumer with the business while the consumer is logged into the account as a verifiable consumer request and providing a mechanism for a consumer who does not maintain an account with the business to request information

through the business's authentication of the consumer's identity, within one year of passage of this title and as needed thereafter.

(b) The Attorney General may adopt additional regulations as necessary to further the purposes of this title.

(c) The Attorney General shall not bring an enforcement action under this title until six months after the publication of the final regulations issued pursuant to this section or July 1, 2020, whichever is sooner.

1798.190 - Intermediate steps or transactions to be disregarded

If a series of steps or transactions were component parts of a single transaction intended from the beginning to be taken with the intention of avoiding the reach of this title, including the disclosure of information by a business to a third party in order to avoid the definition of sell, a court shall disregard the intermediate steps or transactions for purposes of effectuating the purposes of this title.

1798.192 - Void and unenforceable provisions of contract or agreement

Any provision of a contract or agreement of any kind that purports to waive or limit in any way a consumer's rights under this title, including, but not limited to, any right to a remedy or means of enforcement, shall be deemed contrary to public policy and shall be void and unenforceable. This section shall not prevent a consumer from declining to request information from a business, declining to opt out of a business' sale of the consumer's personal information, or authorizing a business to sell the consumer's personal information after previously opting out.

1798.194 - Liberal construction of title

This title shall be liberally construed to effectuate its purposes.

1798.196 - Construction with federal law and California constitution

This title is intended to supplement federal and state law, if permissible, but shall not apply if such application is preempted by, or in conflict with, federal law or the United States or California Constitution.

1798.198 - Operative date pre-condition

(a) Subject to limitation provided in subdivision (b), and in Section 1798.199, this title shall be operative January 1, 2020.

(b) This title shall become operative only if initiative measure No. 17-0039, The Consumer Right to Privacy Act of 2018, is withdrawn from the ballot pursuant to Section 9604 of the Elections Code.

1798.199 - Operative date

Notwithstanding Section 1798.198, Section 1798.180 shall be operative on the effective date of the act adding this section.

Chapter 6 – Where is the conflict?

In June 2018, Privacy advocates celebrated the passage of a historic bill the California Consumer Privacy Act - 2018 that gave residents of that state unprecedented control over how companies use their data. However, their optimism was short lived for no sooner had Governor Jerry Brown signed his approval and the ink barely dry than lobbying groups and trade associations, including several representing the tech industry, sprang into action. Their concerted opposition to the bill started immediately. The 40-strong coalition began pushing for a litany of deep changes that they say would make the law easier to implement before it goes into effect in January 2020. But privacy advocates worry that this level of pressure from powerful businesses will end up gutting the law completely indeed it would be naïve to think the intentions of the lobbyists are otherwise.

"This is their job: to try to make this thing absolutely meaningless. Our job is to say no," says Alastair Mactaggart, chair of the group Californians for Consumer Privacy, which sponsored the ballot initiative that would have ironically circumvented the legislature scrutiny and put the California Consumer Privacy Act to a public vote in November. The opposition, the Committee for California Jobs a proxy for the big Tech companies and other industries lobbied fiercely against the ballot initiative but despite the bill not going to the ballot box - in June, Alastair Mactaggart, withdrew the ballot initiative once the bill, known as AB 375, passed- as they now had a version of the CCPA installed in law.

The reason Alastair Mactaggart and the other sponsors withdrew their Ballot initiative was simply because they had negotiated and managed to draw up with the state lawmakers a compromise, which gave them not all but almost all of their objectives. The details that they forfeit in the compromised bill were simply not worth staging a $100m+ battle over. When you consider that Alastair Mactaggart who had funded the two year campaign at a personal cost of over $2m now had almost everything he wanted in the compromised bill. Then it is fair to see his reticence in wishing to continue the fight against a far wealthier, powerful and influential coalition of businesses when he had little of further value to gain. Furthermore, Alastair Mactaggart, was first and foremost a businessman and not a professional privacy activist so he probably – correctly – assumed that the deal was as good as they could get. He would have known what was difficult but ultimately acceptable to the state business community and the Chamber of Commerce. Hence, any diligent cost versus risk analysis would have made the offer of a compromised privacy bill with the state lawmakers irresistible. Many however believed that to be a strategic mistake.

The reason for the pessimism is that the ballot initiative was Alastair Mactaggart's only real leverage. Once it was withdrawn Mactaggart and the Californians for Consumer Privacy lost almost all relevance. Certainly, they could have threatened to reintroduce the ballot initiative the following year but that would require more expense, labour and time something of huge value to them but resources their opponents had in abundance.

"The new sheriffs showed up and drew a gun. Then they put it down and walked away," Kevin Baker, legislative director of the American Civil Liberties Union in California, says, referring to Alastair Mactaggart's withdrawal of the ballot initiative. "Now that they've done that, and the initiative threat has gone away, we're back to politics as usual."

Mactaggart himself appears to recognise the change in dynamics when he says, "I can talk to people and wave my arms around but the day I signed to give up the petition, I'm like Cinderella back in a pumpkin." That may well be the stark truth but it does not do the story or his efforts justice as Mactaggart had gained the concessions and secured in law almost everything he wanted for the citizens of California.

At the most basic level, the CCPA law allows California residents to gain a measure of control over their personal data, what is collected and how it is used and with whom it is sold or shared. They can also opt-out of their personal data being sold or shared with a third party as well as request deletion. The problem was of course that as attractive as these bundles of rights were to the residents of California they were distressing to the tech industry and a host of other businesses that have personal data at the heart of their business models. Therefore, the belief was that although the Californians for Consumer Privacy and the state lawmakers had agreed a compromised AB 375 bill for privacy and that bill had been unanimously passed in only a few days through both houses of the senate that it wouldn't last due to the concerted efforts of the tech industry. But, it is now down to the state legislators to defend the integrity and spirit of the law against the tech lobbyists who will be determined to pick away at it over 2019 in a bid to render it impotent.

When the opponents of the bill such as the Chamber of Commerce and the other tech groups reluctantly agree to the AB375's speedy passage into law they had done so with the full knowledge that there would be a clean-up process. It was during this clean-up process that the bill would be subjected to detailed review in order to clarify intent, set definitions and generally undergo due diligence albeit after the fact. This of course would be their opportunity to lobby for change and reforms.

The Clean-Up (SB 1121)

As we have previously stated at length the CCPA introduces key privacy rights for consumers and requirements for businesses. The Act was passed quickly by California lawmakers in an effort to remove a ballot initiative of the same name from the November 6, 2018, state-wide ballot. The CCPA's hasty passage resulted in a number of drafting errors and inconsistencies in the law, which SB-1121 seeks to remedy.

There was again just three days left in the legislative session, when the California lawmakers were once again scrambling to vote on a new bill, called SB-1121. The original bill AB-375 had been hastily drafted and then passed in an effort to keep Alastair Mactaggart's initiative off the ballot. The original goal of SB-1121 as a clean-up bill was to deal with typos and other small, technical errors. However, groups like the Chamber of Commerce, Technet, and the Internet Association, which represents companies like Amazon, Google and Facebook, - notable by their absence – as well as about 3 dozen others companies have pushed for significant alterations – 20 pages of them to be precise.

Indeed even organisations such as the Internet Association, which purports to believe in the highest standards for consumer privacy, are coming down strongly against the bill.

"The lack of precise and clear definitions in this legislation will make compliance difficult for companies looking to do the right thing," Robert Callahan, vice president of state government affairs at the Internet Association, said in a statement. "This could lead to serious and costly consequences for internet businesses in

California, which contribute 11.5 percent to the state's overall GDP, as well as every other sector of the economy."

Consequently, in early August, only a month after the passing of CCPA (AB 375), a coalition of nearly 40 organizations, ranging from the banking industry to the film industry to the tech industry's leading lobbying groups, sent a 20-page letter to the lawmakers behind SB-1121, effectively a wish list of changes. While the suggestions weren't ultimately included in the draft of SC 1211, the opposition will hope to introduce more substantive changes in further legislation slated for early 2019. But this should not be misinterpreted as a victory for the proponents of privacy they are a more like an omen of the battle in store in 2019.

Among the most significant proposed changes was a reframing of who the law considers a "consumer." The bill as written applies to all California residents, a provision that industry groups wrote would be "unworkable and have numerous unintended consequences." Instead, trade groups wanted the law only to apply to people whose data was collected because they made a purchase from a business, or used that business's service. They also proposed making it so that only businesses had the right to identify people as consumers, and not the other way around.

The following is how the 40-strong coalition set out their case in a joint letter to Senator Bill Dodds on August 6th 2018. They outlined the issue from their perspective and then provided a proposed solution acceptable to their members – the tech and business community. The following passages are taken directly from the letter to Senator Dodds one of the Co-authors of SB 1121.

Current Definition of Consumer: (g) "Consumer" means a natural person who is a California resident, as defined in Section 17014 of Title 18 of the California Code of Regulations, as that section read on September 1, 2017, however identified, including by any unique identifier.

Issue: The current definition of "consumer" encompasses all California residents, and without clarification could be read as including employees and those involved in business to business interactions. This is contrary to the law's intent as well as its text, including its very title and its multiple references to "consumer data." It would also be unworkable and have numerous unintended consequences. For example, as drafted, an employee accused of sexual harassment could request that complaints about them be expunged (pursuant to the right to delete, Section 1798.105) from company files. In addition, the operational costs of including employees (past and current), job applicants, and other related individuals who do not have a true "consumer" relationship with the business will be exorbitant, and will require many businesses to create separate processes for these individuals. Further, in the context of business to business interactions, the opportunity to delete or opt-out of the disclosure of business data in a business to business transaction could result in fraud and make it impossible to comply with third party due diligence requirements under anti-corruption, anti-money laundering, export control, and Know Your Customer laws.

This would result in a chilling effect on commerce and economic opportunities for businesses based in California, and it would impose millions of dollars in compliance costs on companies that are not handling data in the consumer context.

Our proposed clarified provision would continue to cover information originally obtained in a consumer transaction even if it is held by a credit bureau, data broker, or other businesses. However, it would avoid the problems of including information obtained in employment and business to business situations while aligning the law with the common understanding of who is a consumer.

Proposed Language: Add the following at the end of the definition of "consumer" in Section .140(g): *, to the extent the individual's personal information is obtained as a result of the consumer's purchase or use of a product or service for personal, family, or household purposes. Employees or contractors of a business acting in their role as employee or contractor, as well as commercial or non-residential customers of a business, are not "consumers" for purposes of this title.*

Issue: Title 18, Section 17014 makes the clarification that a resident includes anyone outside the state for temporary reasons. The law is unclear about how a consumer is identified. It states that someone is a California consumer "however identified, including by unique identifier." It is unclear who is identifying the consumer, though, and whether this involves any knowledge on the part of businesses that they have received California consumer data and are therefore subject to the law's requirements.

We propose clarification that it is "the business" that identifies the consumer for the purposes of this definition. This small clarification prevents strict liability, which would have enormous unintended consequences, while furthering the goals of the law.

Proposed Language: Amend this clause in Section .140(g) as follows: *"however identified by the business as such, including by any through a unique identifier."*

Initially this may seem an argument based upon the semantics of the definition of the term consumer within the context of the Act. Nonetheless, this is a very important issue. The target here is to reduce the scope of the bill i.e. to make it only applicable to Californians that have made some kind of transactional interaction such as bought a product or paid for a service with the business. It would not cover marketing surveys, the purchasing of email lists, cold calling or filling out forms online or most importantly all the personal data of friends that was collected by Cambridge Analytics.

"Such a change might seem small, but it would substantially narrow the law's scope," says Mary Stone Ross, who helped draft the ballot initiative as the former president of Californians for Consumer Privacy. "This is significant because it [would] not apply to information that a business does not obtain directly from the consumer," Ross says, like data sold by data brokers or other third parties.

The coalition used the same tactic – seeking precision of a definition – this time personal information to target other major changes. The coalition's issue here was that definition in the context of the act was too broad and ambiguous and hence causes significant compliance issues for business.

Issue: The definition of personal information should be consistent with the notion of an identifiable person, in line with the Obama Administration FTC's definition of "personal information" – including the limitation in the bill that a company does not have to relink or reidentify information in order to comply. The focus of this key definition should be, as it is in California's Shine the Light and CalOPPA laws and every other privacy law and framework, on information that relates to specific individuals. The current definition is so sweeping as to be meaningless. Every piece of data could in theory be randomly "associated with an individual".

Proposed Fixes:

• Clarify that personal information is limited to information "linked or reasonably linkable" to a particular consumer, not information that relates to or could be associated with a consumer, which is any and all information and is too broad to be useful in shaping the definition. "Linked or reasonably linkable" is consistent with the FTC's guidance on privacy.

• Remove references to household, devices, and family. As drafted, one member of a household, whether they are an abusive spouse or a roommate, can access personal information about another member of their household. This runs counter to the privacy goals of AB 375. Also, the term "device" needs to be deleted because devices are often shared by several people and are not personally identifying. Further, the term "devices" is defined to cover all devices (including even industrial devices) so that it far overshoots anything that might identify an individual.

• Clarify that the list of examples of personal data in A-K are a non-exhaustive list of information that may be personal data, but are not always personal information.

• Remove the definition of "probabilistic identifiers" and reference to "probabilistic identifiers" from the definition of "unique personal identifier," which is used in the definition of "personal information."

By definition, probabilistic identifiers are not precise. Businesses would be unable to accurately respond to requests for access or opt out or to verify whether the information they are being asked to disclose actually pertains to the person to whom it would be disclosed. Consequently, it is likely that including probabilistic identifiers (i.e., guesses) would require a business to disclose one individual's personal information to a different individual, in violation of the first individual's privacy.

• Remove reference to inferences and tendencies, which are guesses based on patterns of behavior.

In addition to the ambiguity of these terms and the ambiguity of how they would be applied, these terms could apply to insights developed through the use of proprietary algorithms and other AI processes. Allowing inferences and tendencies to be included under the definition of personal information will give consumers access to and deletion rights over insights developed with proprietary tools, which creates the potential for reverse engineering.

• Remove references to Professional or Employment-Related Information, in 1798.140(o)(1)(I).

This phrase is written so broadly it could be read to confer rights to employees vis-à-vis their employers with respect to their personnel records, and it is not necessary because all identifiable information will be personal data.

• Clarify the scope of the definition of "personal information" to explicitly exclude deidentified, aggregate, pseudonymized consumer information. Pseudonymized information, like deidentified and aggregate consumer information, cannot readily be identified with a particular individual, and is a privacy enhancing process. In order to make the definition of "personal information" consistent with the notion of an identifiable person, none of these terms should be included in it. The current law, due to a drafting error, fails to exempt even de-identified or aggregate data from the definition of "personal information," instead exempting it from the definition of "publicly available data."

In seeking a more precise or narrower definition of personal identifiable information and relevant exceptions to the rule the coalition raises many very pertinent points. For instance they stress the point that identifiable information must be "linked or reasonably linkable" to a particular consumer, not information that relates to or could be associated with a consumer. Similarly they stress the issues with determining a device as being personally identifiable as there are many instances where they clearly are not. Nonetheless, their point that personal identifiable information is no longer such when de-identified is valid. This reasoning is in line with other privacy legislations such as the GDPR which encourages businesses to store and process anonymised or pseudo-anonymised personal identifiable information. The reason being is that in an encrypted or redacted state it is worthless as personally identifiable information. Furthermore, they have a valid point when it comes to excluding data produced by inferences and tendencies as being personal identified information, not because they are inaccurate but because the product, which is often the output from an algorithm or risk assessment process or similar isn't owned by the consumer.

Another similar issue raised by the 40-strong coalition was the case of;

Remove Requirement that Businesses Should Identify "Specific Pieces of Information" about Consumers

Issue: AB 375 does not explain or define what it means by "specific pieces" of personal information, and providing certain information, such as a consumer's social security number or driver's license number, in response to such requests creates unnecessary risks to both the security of the consumer's information and the business' ability to protect such information. There is also the risk of inadvertent disclosure to a fraudster posing as the consumer. Additionally, to the extent it requires a business to research and re-associate every data element with in the definition of "personal information" with an identifiable individual, it is unworkable.

This change is needed to resolve contradictory sections in the bill, and give effect to exemptions in the bill that clarify a business is not required to relink or reidentify data (see 1798.145, 1798.100, and 1798.110).

A business cannot provide "specific pieces of information" without relinking or reidentifying data in order to match it to the person making the request. Indeed, Section 1798.130 already reflects this by directing a business to comply with 1798.110 by identifying "by category or categories" of information.

Requiring a business to maintain records in a form that directly identifies individuals in order to be able to respond to a request for "specific pieces of information" would undermine privacy and these other provisions of AB 375. In order to facilitate Internet commerce while safeguarding consumer privacy and security, businesses typically maintain consumer information in pseudonymized form. This means that information is not directly linked to an identifiable consumer, but it does not necessarily meet the high standard that the FTC has set for information that is "deidentified." Directly linking data contravenes best practices for data security and results in a lower standard of protection for consumer personal information. AB 375 already expands transparency enormously, and this provision is unnecessary from the perspective of increasing transparency and protecting consumers.

Proposed Language:

1798.100(a) – strike reference to "specific pieces"; strike 1798.110(a)(5) and (c)(5) entirely

1798.100(a) A consumer shall have the right to request that a business that collects a consumer's personal information disclose to that consumer the categories of personal information the business has collected.

Whereas the original bill requires companies to share specific pieces of data, the industry groups prefer to draw the line at "categories of personal information." Again this seems at first glance to be a seemingly logical and sensible approach to making sure the personal identifiable information stored by a business about a consumer is encrypted or redacted. Therefore, providing the consumer with a disclosure of data based upon categories seems logical, such as a disclosure that they hold the consumer's credit card and bank details. This is because the specific data i.e. the card number and expiry date should not be visible or accessible to anyone in the business, including developers, database administrators or customer service agents. The problem is though how can the consumer check that the data held about them is correct – many issues arise due to businesses holding out of date personal data about consumers. Hence, there is a necessity for consumers to be able to access and verify the data that is stored and this requires encryption and providing consumers secure access to their personal data – but that is expensive and something businesses wish to avoid. Hence perhaps why the right to validation and correction is not part of the CCPA.

However, moving on from the semantic challenges of what constitutes a consumer and personal information. There is another major anomaly within the law which includes language that would prevent a business from discriminating against people by, say, charging them inordinate fees or reducing the level of service if they opt out of data collection. But prohibiting blanket discrimination is too broad for the business groups, who want to add a caveat specifying that they may not "unreasonably" discriminate. But the real confusion arises when a seemingly contradictory provision is made, which discusses and does not rule out offering consumers incentives for the sale of their data. But how do these co-exist, for on one-hand we have a rule forbidding the discrimination against those that choose to exercise their rights and opt-out. However on the other-hand for consumers that choose to do nothing – as there is no opt-in - can legitimately be rewarded financially with the caveat being "A business shall not use financial incentive practices that are unjust, unreasonable, coercive, or usurious in nature." Unhappy with this restriction the industry groups proposed striking the words "financial", "unjust" and "unreasonable" and this is how they made their case:

Issue: The exemptions from the law's non-discrimination obligation are inconsistent and confusing. The exemption under (a)(2) includes language about value to the consumer of their own data, rather than the value of the consumer's data to the business offering the service. Moreover, the financial incentives provision creates two inconsistent "reasonably related" and "directly related" standards. Also, there must be an exception for data that is reasonably necessary to provide the product or service. Otherwise, this provision would be impossible to comply with where a user has opted out of data processing necessary to provide them with a particular service or feature, such as where a user opts out of data sharing with a third party that is needed to provide content like music, apps, or games.

These features and programs are typically offered on an opt-in basis, with notice to the consumer that information will be collected and used. These programs are popular with consumers and often provide access to low-cost or free services, such as free WiFi. A confusing set of requirements imposed on such programs could significantly hamper business' ability to offer them and consumers' ability to benefit from them.

Proposed Language:

1798.125

(a) (1) A business shall not unreasonably discriminate against a consumer because the consumer exercised any of the consumer's rights under this title, including, but not limited to, by:

(A) Denying goods or services to the consumer.

(B) Charging different prices or rates for goods or services, including through the use of discounts or other benefits or imposing penalties.

(C) Providing a different level or quality of goods or services to the consumer, if the consumer exercises the consumer's rights under this title.

(D) Suggesting that the consumer will receive a different price or rate for goods or services or a different level or quality of goods or services.

(2) Nothing in this subdivision prohibits a business from charging a consumer a different price or rate, or from providing a different level or quality of goods or services to the consumer, if that difference is reasonably related to the value provided to the consumer by the consumer's data.

(b) (1) A business may offer incentives, including but not limited to, payments to consumers as compensation for the sale or retention of personal information, or the retention of personal information. A business may also offer a different price, rate, level, or quality of goods or services to the consumer, including offering its good or service for no fee, if that price or difference is reasonably related to the value provided to the business by the consumer's data.

(2) A business that offers any incentives pursuant to subdivision (a), shall notify consumers of the incentives pursuant to Section 1798.135.

(3) A business may enter a consumer into an incentive program only if the consumer gives the business prior opt-in consent after notice which clearly describes the material terms of the incentive program, and which may be revoked by the consumer at any time.

But as spokesperson for Californians for Consumer Privacy, Ross said "If these changes are permitted, a business could offer financial incentives that are unjust or unreasonable. Weakening these non-discrimination provisions, she says, could "turn privacy into a commodity that will disproportionately burden the poor."

However it would be wrong to suggest that all the points raised in opposition to the bill were anti-privacy in nature as there was much bipartisan agreement, one such example was on the granularity of the opt-out option. As the business coalition put forward:

Allow Consumers the Option to Choose the Types of "Sales" They Want to Opt Out of, Instead of Mandating Only One "All or Nothing" Opt-out

Issue: Currently, AB 375 could be construed to require a business to apply a consumer's opt-out of one type of sale of personal information, such as third-party cookies on a website, to another type of sale, such as a joint marketing email campaign. This could have unintended consequences that harm consumers.

For example, if a consumer opts out of receiving online targeted ads resulting from the use of third-party cookies, unless the law is clarified, he or she might also inadvertently be deprived of special discounts and promotions for existing or new services that could save them money. From an operational perspective, it would also require fundamental changes to the existing online self-regulatory, opt-out mechanisms. A prior version of the ballot initiative contained language designed to give consumers these expanded choices, and similar language could be added to Section 1798.120 as follows:

Proposed Language: (d) A consumer's opt-out request can be limited to specific types of personal information, specific types of sales of personal information, or sales of personal information to categories of third parties. A business that has received direction from a consumer not to sell the consumer's personal information or, in the case of a minor consumer's personal information has not received consent to sell the minor consumer's personal information shall be prohibited from selling the consumer's personal information unless the consumer subsequently provides affirmative authorization for the sale of the consumer's personal information.

Indeed this is a provision that the pro-privacy non-profit organisation Electronic Frontier Foundation have also been actively lobbying for as they also want finer granularity of choice, though preferably through an opt-in mechanism. But it does go to illustrate that it was not as antagonistic and confrontational as it might at first be envisaged.

Nonetheless, there are still points that are considered sacrosanct by both parties. The final sticking point, particularly for the tech giants, was the law's handling of data collected for the purposes of advertising. While the law prohibits users from opting out of advertising altogether, it does allow them to opt out of the sale of their personal information to a third party. This is of course an irrelevance to Google and Facebook as they do not sell personal data to third parties. Nonetheless, the industry still were keen to create an exception for information that's sold for the purposes of targeted advertising, where the users' identities aren't disclosed to that third party. This was of course not the kind of granularity of opt-out that pro-privacy groups such as the EFF were endorsing. Consequently, despite being in broad agreement over the desirability for a granular opt-out mechanism the privacy groups including the ACLU and EFF vehemently opposed this proposal, as did Alastair Mactaggart. They argued that such a carve-out would create too big a loophole for businesses and undermine consumers' right to truly know everything businesses had collected on them.

"I was surprised they were this blatant, this early," Alastair Mactaggart, says. "I expected this attack in 2019, but not in August 2018, two months after we passed the bill in the first place."

The industry groups' lobbyists failed to get that amendment into the SB 1121 bill this time around. But Alastair Mactaggart and others expect to fight this battle all over again in 2019.

Room for Improvement

Where there is consensus across the board is that the privacy bill is certainly not perfect. The ACLU, for one, criticized the CCPA for the exclusion of a provision in the ballot initiative that would have given people the right to sue companies for violating their data privacy rights. The bill instead leaves enforcement up to the Attorney General, except in the case of a data breach. In response, the Attorney General Xavier Becerra proposed his own list of changes to the law including the restoration of people's ability to sue.

Nonetheless, as the bill was being finalized, all sides did agree to some tweaks, like clarifying language that would protect data collected through clinical trials and other health-related information. Another change ensures that information collected by journalists remains safeguarded. Even the Attorney General didn't get everything he asked for but the legislature did agree to provide his office with an additional six months to implement enforcement regulations.

The Electronic Frontier Foundation also concedes the law needs more substantive work. The organization wants to change the bill so that consumers would be able to opt-in to data collection, rather than opt-out. This mechanism requires a consumer's affirmative action to provide consent and hence establishes consumer privacy as the default. The principle being that doing nothing (silence) must not be considered as providing consent. Also, codifying this opt-in measure would allow CCPA to co-exist with GDPR and make technical compliance easier for business. The EFF also wants to ensure the law applies not just to businesses that buy and sell data, but data they share with third parties, often under the pretext of research. But that was the flaw that enabled some app developers to gain access to Facebook and Google+ users' friends' data for years.

For now, all sides at least agree that SB-1121 was effectively merely a stopgap. The fact that the tech cartels and the business coalitions didn't get their way this time certainly doesn't mean they will simply accept defeat. The business groups will regroup, hone their strategy and tactics as well as intensifying their lobbying of the senate. This time around the business group appeared to go in with all guns blazing but with a scattershot approach and as Lee Tien, senior staff attorney at the EFF, says, "The business groups' ham-fisted effort to jam so many changes through in a matter of months is counterproductive." However he does acknowledge that they will likely refine their approach over the next year. "There will be battles over the definition of consumer and personal information, and we're prepared to talk seriously about those definitions," he says. "But that can't happen in any kind of responsible, grown-up way, in a short period of time."

Next year's legislative session will likely see new bills with even more serious changes proposed by influential industries. The opponents of the bill will have several chances over the next year to succeed, and they'll be back for sure just better prepared and focused.

"One of the reasons why AB 375 passed unanimously is everyone knew there'd be a clean-up bill, and they had plenty of time to lobby to get their changes through," adds Ross of Californians for Consumer Privacy, who opposed pulling the ballot initiative.

SB 1121 passes into law

On August 31, 2018, the California State Legislature passed SB-1121, a bill that delays enforcement of the California Consumer Privacy Act of 2018 ("CCPA") and makes other amendments to the CCPA, which are primarily technical but with a few substantive changes to the law. The bill was approved and signed by the

Governor on the 24th September 2018. The provisions of the CCPA will become operative on January 1, 2020.

Key SB-1121 amendments to the CCPA include:

Enforcement of the Act:

The bill extends by six months the deadline for the California Attorney General ("AG") to draft and adopt the law's implementing regulations, from January 1, 2020, to July 1, 2020. (CCPA § 1798.185(a)).

The bill delays the AG's ability to bring enforcement actions under the CCPA until six months after publication of the implementing regulations or July 1, 2020, whichever comes first. (CCPA § 1798.185(c)).

The bill limits the civil penalties the AG can impose to $2,500 for each violation of the CCPA or up to $7,500 per each intentional violation, and states that a violating entity will be subject to an injunction. (CCPA § 1798.155(b)).

Definition of "personal information":

The CCPA includes a number of enumerated examples of "personal information" ("PI"), including IP address, geolocation data and web browsing history. The amendment clarifies that the listed examples would constitute PI only if the data "identifies, relates to, describes, is capable of being associated with, or could be reasonably linked, directly or indirectly, with a particular consumer or household." (CCPA § 1798.140(o)(1)).

Private right of action:

The amendments clarify that a consumer may bring an action under the CCPA only for a business's alleged failure to "implement and maintain reasonable security procedures and practices" that results in a data breach. (CCPA § 1798.150(c)).

The bill removes the requirement that a consumer notify the AG once the consumer has brought an action against a business under the CCPA, and eliminates the AG's ability to instruct a consumer to not proceed with an action. (CCPA § 1798.150(b)).

GLBA, DDPA, CIPA exemptions:

The original text of the CCPA exempted information subject to the Gramm-Leach-Bliley Act ("GLBA") and Driver's Privacy Protection Act ("DPPA"), only to the extent the CCPA was "in conflict" with either statute. The bill removes the "in conflict" qualification and clarifies that data collected, processed, sold or disclosed pursuant to the GLBA, DPPA or the California Information Privacy Act is exempt from the CCPA's requirements. The revisions also exempt such information from the CCPA's private right of action provision. (CCPA §§ 1798.145(e), (f)).

Health information:

Health care providers: The bill adds an exemption for HIPAA-covered entities and providers of health care governed by the Confidentiality of Medical Information Act, "to the extent the provider or covered entity maintains patient information in the same manner as medical information or protected health information," as described in the CCPA. (CCPA § 1798.145(c)(1)(B)).

PHI:

The bill expands the category of exempted protected health information ("PHI") governed by HIPAA and the Health Information Technology for Economic and Clinical Health Act to include PHI collected by both covered entities and business associates. The original text did not address business associates. (CCPA § 1798.145(c)(1)(A)).

Clinical trial data:

The bill adds an exemption for "information collected as part of a clinical trial" that is subject to the Federal Policy for the Protection of Human Subjects (also known as the Common Rule) and is conducted in accordance with specified clinical practice guidelines. (CCPA § 1798.145(c)(1)(C)).

Notice of right of deletion:

The original text of the CCPA stated that a business must disclose on its website or in its privacy policy a consumer's right to request the deletion of her PI. The bill modifies this requirement, stating that a business must disclose the right to deletion "in a form that is reasonably accessible to consumers." (CCPA § 1798.105(b)).

First Amendment protection:

The bill adds a provision to the CCPA, which states that the rights afforded to consumers and obligations imposed on businesses under the CCPA do not apply if they "infringe on the non-commercial activities of a person or entity" as described in Art. I, Section 2(b) of the California constitution, which addresses activities related to the free press. This provision is designed to prevent First Amendment challenges to the law. (CCPA § 1798.150(k)).

Preemption:

The bill adds to the CCPA's preemption clause that the law will not apply in the event its application is preempted by, or in conflict with, the U.S. Constitution. The CCPA previously referenced only the California Constitution. (CCPA § 1798.196).

Certain provisions of the CCPA supersede and preempt laws adopted by local entities regarding the collection and sale of a consumer's PI by a business. The bill makes such provisions of the Act operative on the date the bill becomes effective.

The California State Legislature is expected to consider more substantive changes to the law when it reconvenes in January 2019.

The CCPA becomes effective January 1, 2020, though practically, businesses will need to start data mapping and recordkeeping on January 1, 2019, to be able to be in compliance upon the effective date. The legislature already started the initial clean-up process of potentially amending the CCPA through SB-1121 that would amend the CCPA in the following modest ways:

- A business would not be required to disclose a consumer's deletion right on its website or in its online privacy policy(ies). Rather, it must provide notice "in a form that is reasonably accessible to consumers." Thus, a business could provide notice through its privacy policy but is not required to.
- Adds a statement that the rights and obligations under the CCPA do not apply if they infringe on a business' non-

commercial speech rights. This is a further attempt to guard against a First Amendment challenge to the law.

- Adds a sentence clarifying that the private right of action only applies to "violations" that are security incidents as described in CA CIVIL CODE.
- Adds that the CCPA will not apply if its application is pre-empted by or is in conflict with the US Constitution. The CCPA, as passed, already stated that it will not apply if its application is pre-empted by or is in conflict with federal law or the California Constitution.
- Makes various grammatical, technical and clarifying changes to the CCPA. For example, it would change "business'" to "business's" and "opt out" to "opt-out."

The 8/24 Amendment proposes other material changes, such as:

- Prohibiting application of the Act to personal information collected, processed, sold, or disclosed pursuant to the federal Gramm-Leach-Bliley Act (governing financial institutions) or the CA Financial Information Privacy Act, or protected health information collected by a covered entity or business associate governed by the federal Health Insurance Portability and Accountability Act or medical information governed by the CA Confidentiality of Medical Information Act. This expands existing carve outs.
- Further clarifies that the private right of action is limited to the type of data security incident defined in subsection (a) of Section 1798.150 and not any other violations of "any other sections of this title."
- Revises the definition of personal information to clarify that data that falls into the categories of personal information

described will only be personal information if "it identifies, relates to, describes, is capable of being associated with, or could be reasonably linked, directly or indirectly, with a particular consumer or household." In other words, data falling into one of the specified categories is not per se personal information.

- Changes the civil penalty provisions available to the Attorney General by (i) making them independent of Section 17206 of the Business and Professions Code; and (ii) providing that penalty for each violation can be up to $7500 regardless of intent (intent currently required to exceed $2500 per violation).

- Removes the one year requirement for the Attorney General to establish certain rules and procedures (e.g., opt-out), puts a deadline of July 1, 2020 on the Attorney General to adopt regulations furthering the purpose of the Act, and limits enforcement by the Attorney General until six months thereafter, or July 1, 2020, whichever is sooner.

- Makes the pre-emption of local laws immediate

A summary guide to the CCPA

The Act gives "consumers" (defined as natural persons who are California residents) four basic rights in relation to their personal information:

- the right to know, through a general privacy policy and with more specifics available upon request, what personal information a business has collected about them, where it was sourced from, what it is being used for, whether it is being disclosed or sold, and to whom it is being disclosed or sold;

- the right to "opt-out" of allowing a business to sell their personal information to third parties (or, for consumers who are under 16 years old, the right not to have their personal information sold absent their or their parent's, opt-in);
- the right to have a business delete their personal information, with some exceptions; and
- the right to receive equal service and pricing from a business, even if they exercise their privacy rights under the Act.

The Act's provisions are designed to put these rights into practice.

The Act requires that companies make certain disclosures to consumers via their privacy policies, or otherwise at the time the personal data is collected. For example, businesses need to disclose proactively the existence and nature of consumers' rights under the Act, the categories of personal information they collect, the purposes for which that personal information is collected, and the categories of personal information that it sold or disclosed in the preceding 12 months. In terms of compliance, these provisions will require companies to determine what personal data they are collecting from individuals and for what purposes, and to update their privacy policies every 12 months to make the disclosures the Act requires.

Companies that sell consumer data to third parties will need to disclose that practice and give consumers the ability to opt out of the sale by supplying a link titled "Do Not Sell My Personal Information" on the business's home page. This is known as the right to "opt-out." The Act further provides that a business must not sell the personal information of consumers younger than 16 years of age without that consumer's affirmative consent (or, for consumers younger than 13 years of age, without the affirmative consent of the consumer's parent or guardian). This is known as the right to "opt-in."

Consumers also have the right to request certain information from businesses, including, for example, the sources from which a business collected the consumer's personal information, the specific pieces of personal information it collected about the consumer, and the third parties with which it shared that information. The Act requires businesses to provide at least two means for consumers to submit requests for disclosure including, at minimum, a toll-free telephone number and Web site. Additionally, businesses will have to disclose the requested information free of charge within 45 days of the receipt of a consumer's request, subject to possible extensions of this time frame. Companies therefore will need to determine how they can monitor their data sharing practices and marshal the requested information within a short period of time pursuant to a data subject's request.

The Act also forbids businesses from "discriminating" against consumers for exercising their privacy rights under the Act. More specifically, that means businesses cannot deny goods or services, charge different prices for goods or services, or provide a different quality of goods or services to those consumers who exercise their privacy rights. However, the Act does permit businesses to charge a different price, or provide a different level of service, to a customer "if that difference is reasonably related to the value provided to the consumer by the consumer's data." It also is worth noting that businesses are permitted to offer financial or other incentives to consumers for the collection, sale, or deletion of personal information, subject to specific conditions and notice requirements.

▌Where are other potential issues buried

Lobbyists for both industry and consumer groups are pushing for a variety of changes. However, as the legislative history of both AB-375 and SB-1121 indicates the ballot initiative sponsors have promised to revive the initiative if CCPA is diluted. The EFF and other groups are pushing not to water down, but to further expand, consumer rights under the CCPA. For instance, the EFF's proposals include expanding the private right of action to any breach of the CCPA's obligations, including privacy transparency and choice requirements. The legislative history of the CCPA and reports of what went on behind the scenes to reach the compromise indicate that a very narrow private right of action was a key issue for industry, and AB 375's authors accepted that as fundamental to the compromise.

There are still major issues that businesses will require clarification and guidance. The advertising industry in particular will require resolution of outstanding issues regarding the precise definition of personal information, de-identified and aggregate data, disclosure of specific or categorised information, data portability, alternatives to an all-or-nothing opt-out of sales, clarifications on incentive and loyalty programs, and issues regarding interest-based advertising.

If we consider each in turn then we start with the most likely source of ambiguity as well as the richest prize that of the definition of personal information. The CCPA regulates "personal information," broadly defined as "information that identifies, relates to, describes, is capable of being associated with or could reasonably be linked, directly or indirectly with a particular consumer or household." This broad definition includes a wide variety of information collected both online and offline. The problem is though that with such broad scope it will be hard to identify information about a person that is not in some way capable of being associated with a particular consumer or household. For instance, demographic data alone (e.g., gender, profession, race) is capable of being associated with a person, but alone, it will not reasonably enable their identification or be reasonably linked to a specific person. While a broad definition is more convenient with respect to providing notice of what data is collected, disclosed or sold, or applied to opt-out, portability and deletion rights, it is likely practically unworkable as being personally identifiable information (PII). This problem is made worse by the CCPA's ambiguities regarding deidentified data and aggregate consumer information.

The definition of Personal Information under the CCPA does not include publicly available information. "Publicly available" is defined as "information that is lawfully made available from federal, state or local government records". Further, under the Act, information is not "publicly available" if that data is used for a purpose that is not compatible with the purpose for which the data is maintained and made available in the government records or for which it is publicly maintained. This is an important point as many businesses use publicly available data for commercial purposes that are not compatible with the original purpose for posting. Also excluded as not being personal information is deidentified data and aggregate consumer information, suggesting that these types of data are intended to be excluded from the definition of both personal and publicly available information, but this is unclear as the law is currently worded. However, Section 1798.145(a)(5) provides that "[t]he obligations imposed on businesses by this title shall not restrict a business's ability to ... collect, use, retain, sell or disclose consumer information that is deidentified or in the aggregate consumer information." This would seem sufficient to remove deidentified and aggregate consumer information from the data applicable to deletion, portability and "do not sell" rights.

However, the other obligations regarding personal information would seem to apply unless the definition of personal information is not clarified to exclude deidentified and aggregate consumer information across the board.

Another ambiguity regarding what is and is not personal information has to do with device identifiers. The definition of personal information is tied to a "particular consumer or household," but a "device" is not included in the definition. However, Unique IDs and Probabilistic IDs, both of which are typically tied to a device are included as examples of personal information and they are also categories that personal information is to be grouped in for reporting purposes. Further, the definition of aggregate consumer information excludes information that is linkable to a device. This raises an interesting conundrum, are browser IDs, cookie IDs, IEMI and other unique identifiers used to identify a device, or a pseudonymous user, personal information or will that be considered deidentified? This is particularly relevant given the personal information deletion right. Under a broad interpretation of the Act, such a deletion request could potentially require the deletion of cookies, other device IDs, other unique identifiers and related usage data for many of the purposes for which a business would typically use them. Further it is unlikely these use cases will be included in the exceptions of the rights for deletion provision.

The CCPA requires a business that collects a consumer's personal information to, at or before the point of collection, inform consumers as to the categories of personal information to be collected and the purposes for which the categories of personal information will be used. A business cannot collect additional categories of personal information or use personal information collected for additional purposes without providing the consumer with such notice. No guidance is given on whether disclosure in a publicly posted privacy policy is sufficient notice. This is particularly relevant when the collection takes place in a context remote from where the privacy policy is posted. For instance, collection includes buying, renting, obtaining or receiving personal information indirectly or passively and/or from a third party. Other than in a publicly posted privacy policy, how could a business make the required disclosures prior to a third-party transfer where the business has no touchpoint with the data subject? While the recipient business could contractually require the disclosing business to provide the notice prior to its collection, that would not seem to meet the technical requirements of the statute.

Under the CCPA, "selling," is defined as "selling, renting, releasing, disclosing, disseminating, making available, transferring or otherwise communicating a consumer's personal information to another business or a third party for monetary or valuable consideration."

However, a business does not "sell" personal information under the CCPA when a consumer uses or directs the business to intentionally disclose personal information or uses the business to intentionally interact with a third party, provided the third party does not also sell the personal information, unless that disclosure would be consistent with the provisions of the Act. This could present a problem for things like social media plug-ins, where the business implementing the plug-in on its site is arguably obtaining the value of the use of the plug-in (e.g., registering likes of the business or sharing messages about the business). This could be addressed by requiring monetary consideration to rise to the level of sale and/or providing for other than an all-or-nothing opt-out requirement.

Consumers have the right to equal service and price, meaning that a business cannot discriminate against a consumer because the consumer exercised any of their rights under the CCPA, subject to certain exceptions. However, a diluted version of this right has crept in and now a business can charge a consumer a different price or rate, or provide a different level or quality of goods or services if the difference in price, rate or quality is "reasonably related to the value provided to the Consumer by the Consumer's data." How can it be determined even subjectively the value to a consumer of the differentiation in product or service let alone the value the consumer places on their own personal data.

The private right of action

The CCPA removed the right of private action for violations of rights within the Act but there does remain a narrow private right of action under the CCPA. However, certain conditions must be met such as, "[a]ny Consumer whose non-encrypted or non-redacted Personal Information, as defined in Section 1798.81.5(d)(1)(A), is subject to an unauthorized access and exfiltration, theft, or disclosure as a result of the businesses violation of the duty to implement and maintain reasonable security procedures and practices appropriate to the nature of the information to protect the personal information may institute" a private right of action for any of the following: (a) damages not less than $100 and not greater than $750 per consumer per incident, or actual damages, whichever is greater, (b) injunctive or declaratory relief and (c) any other relief the court deems proper, IF all the following requirements are met:

(1) Before initiating any action on an individual or class-wide basis, the consumer provides the business 30 days' written notice identifying the specific provisions of the CCPA that the consumer alleges have been or are being violated, and a 30-day opportunity to cure;

(2) A consumer bringing an action notifies the CaAG within 30 days that the action has been filed; and

(3) The CaAG, upon receiving such notice, shall, within 30 days, do one of the following:

• Notify the consumer bringing the action of the CaAG's intent to prosecute an action against the violation. If the CaAG does not prosecute within six months, the consumer may proceed with the action;

• Refrain from acting within the 30 days, allowing the consumer bringing the action to proceed; or

• Notify the consumer bringing the action that the consumer shall not proceed with the action.

Pursuant to the Act, in assessing the amount of statutory damages, the court shall consider any one or more of the relevant circumstances presented by any of the parties to the case, including, but not limited to, the nature and seriousness of the misconduct, the number of violations, the persistence of the misconduct, the length of time over which the misconduct occurred, the willfulness of the defendant's misconduct and the defendant's assets, liabilities, and net worth. A business's timely cure, however, will preclude statutory damages.

As passed, the CCPA has no express duty regarding data security but having said that the CCPA's limited private right of action is for security breaches of some of the types of data elements that would trigger a notification requirement under CA Civil Code Title 1.81.

However as a consumer's CCPA cause of action is limited to data security failures following a breach, it is unclear how a business could retrospectively cure a past breach. Does this mean that all that would be necessary is to prospectively cure the security inadequacies?

Current and anticipated business models should be reviewed under the CCPA, keeping in mind that the new law is subject to change and modification (not to mention other states laws will most likely follow, and federal legislation and regulation is being considered).

The CCPA is part of a general trend for more regulation regarding privacy and security. January 1, 2020 may seem far away, but compliance will take time to make the required investments, processes and procedures, even as we wait for further clarification and additional laws. It is notable that there is already some push towards federal legislation that would create uniformity instead of a "patchwork" of states laws. In any event, there will be common themes to most of these laws and companies will need to consider taking an "enterprise wide" approach.

Unlike the GDPR, the CCPA does not require a data privacy officer. Many companies that are consumer-data "heavy" either have or are realizing that they need a true, privacy "office." If a business does not have a privacy office, now is a good time to create one and also create the processes needed to comply with the CCPA.

The CCPA if nothing else will provide businesses with an opportunity to assess and revaluate some of their "best practices" in terms of business models, policies, practices and even the negotiation of privacy and security provisions. For example, assessing the effects on the business model of even some of the subtle changes in the definition of what is considered "personal information" and what is "publicly available" is a good example, as those terms are defined under the CCPA.

Furthermore, the CCPA is one of the first major pieces of legislation regulating "geolocation." Now again it will be interesting for businesses to revaluate their business models to determine how they use geolocation data. Many new businesses producing mobile apps and IoT devices however those businesses using that data (including linking to generic websites that track location) will need to consider the CCPA, and especially how to provide opt-out mechanisms.

Moreover, the definition of personal information also includes "inferences" drawn from any of the terms that are included in the definition of personal information under the CCPA to create a profile about a consumer reflecting the consumer's "preferences, characteristics, psychological trends, preferences, predispositions, behaviour, attitudes, intelligence, abilities, and aptitudes." Now in the age of Big Data, Machine Learning and Artificial Intelligence there are companies whose sole existence is based on making inferences and tracking behaviours. A business cannot escape the CCPA merely because of the derivative nature of the personal information that was originally captured—it also includes inferences made by the data captured. This is a concept that is often negotiated in a technology deal both in terms ownership and use of "inferences," but which now has more direction with respect to the CCPA. The removal or exemption of Inferences and Tendencies from the list of examples of personal information is likely to be one of the major battlefield objectives in 2019.

While there are other things to consider, a final thought is how the CCPA treats "deidentified" information in order to take advantage of an exception to compliance with the CCPA. The CCPA does not restrict a business's ability to collect, use, retain, sell, or disclose consumer information that is deidentified or in the aggregate consumer information. As practitioners are aware, just because information is "deidentified" does not mean that there are third parties that cannot "reidentify" such information. This is where having contracts with third parties that prohibit the future re-identification of data becomes crucial as that under the CCPA is deemed a sufficient control.

The California legislature passed AB 375, the California Consumer Privacy Act of 2018, on Thursday, June 28, 2018, effective January 1, 2020 (the "CCPA"). The CCPA law follows a trend in the law and market towards greater transparency and protection of consumers' personal information. The European Union kicked-off the major legal trend of laws, passing the General Data Protection Regulation ("GDPR") that became effective on May 25, 2018. The GDPR is the EU's response to the plethora of data breaches and the publics' concerns over privacy. In a similar manner the CCPA is a major piece of privacy legislation addressing the same concerns. The California legislature further explained its motivation, noting that: "[I]n March 2018, it came to light that tens of millions of people had their personal data misused by a data mining firm called Cambridge Analytica. A series of congressional hearings highlighted that our personal information may be vulnerable to misuse when shared on the Internet. As a result, our desire for privacy controls and transparency in data practices is heightened."

The California Attorney General is charged with enforcing and promulgating regulations to help explain and clarify or even "modify" the CCPA, and businesses are also encouraged to request guidance. It is highly likely that amendments to the CCPA itself will be made prior to its effective date. Having said that, the CCPA outlines some basic tenets giving Californians' the right to privacy by ensuring the following:

- to know what personal information is being collected about them.
- to know whether their personal information is sold or disclosed and to whom.
- to say no to the sale of personal information.
- To request data about them be deleted.
- to access their personal information.
- to equal service and price, even if they exercise their privacy rights.

Compliance with this new act could prove to be tricky until more details are released by the lawmakers because there are many anomalies, ambiguities and downright contradictions that must be addressed. Of course, companies that have already moved towards becoming GDPR compliant are probably well ahead on the road to compliance. At least with regards the core disciplines of data governance, data mapping and privacy assessments, but the CCPA is different from the GDPR in many respects.

Avoid the CCPA's jurisdiction

Nonetheless, the CCPA just as with the GDPR can be accommodated relatively easily by most businesses. This is because the CCPA focuses exclusively on data collection and privacy, and is roughly in line with the provisions of GDPR on those issues. Hence the easiest and least onerous method for compliance is not to fall under the regulations jurisdiction in the first place. To understand how this is accomplished the criteria for companies that have to honour the rights granted to Californians are:

- Businesses with annual gross revenues of at least $25 million
- Data brokers and other businesses that *buy, receive, sell, or share* the personal information of 50,000 or more consumers, households, or devices
- Business that get the *majority of their annual revenue* from *selling* consumers' personal information.

As can be seen by the criteria above the focus is on data brokerage i.e. companies that *buy, receive, sell, or share* personal information. For companies that are data brokers or data brokerage is the majority source of revenue there is no escaping the focus of the CCPA. However, companies that are not primarily data brokers and do not generate more than 50% of their revenue through the sale of personal information should contemplate the real value of *buying, receiving, selling, or sharing* personal information to their business model. A business model analysis will surface the true business value – if any – for the *buying, receiving, selling, or sharing* of personal information. Interestingly, due to the hype in recent years regarding the value of data many companies collect and store data for little practical reason. Consequently, the vast trove of stored data goes unprocessed or is traded as a by-product. In either case it is more a liability than a benefit. Hence, following a few best practices for data collection may be the simplest solution to the rigours of compliance. Some best practices regard personal data collection and management that are informed by the consumer privacy act are:

- Only collect data that you have a clear immediate use for. Data is power, but it's also an increasingly liability. Limit that liability by being selective about what data you save, particularly when it comes to personally identifiable information (PII).

- If your business must collect and store personal information then ensure it is deidentified through encryption or redaction. Anonymisation or pseudonymisation of personal data can mitigate the consequences and penalties for even serious breaches.
- Reconsider whether you need to use third-party data. The CCPA gives consumers the right to know "the categories of sources from which the personal information is collected." Trading in consumers' personal data will eventually come to light via a CCPA request. Thus, if the company would be uncomfortable explaining that to customers, then you might want to halt the practice.
- Re-evaluate the data fields on forms and profiles. The CCPA is part of a clear shift toward data transparency that spurs businesses to make greater use of data that is collected directly from their customers. Is there information that you're currently getting via third-parties that you could ask customers and prospects for directly?
- Create a mechanism that can delete a consumer's information, when requested. Both CCPA and the GDPR stipulate that consumers have the right to be forgotten and request that any data your company has on them be deleted. There are some caveats on what data a business can retain for legal, compliance, and business reasons, but a mechanism must exist to quickly delete all other personal information about a consumer.
- Don't sell information about your customers or users. If you're going to sell user information to other companies,

the CCPA requires you to keep a record of all sales of data for 12 months and provide a "clear and conspicuous" link on your website with the call-to-action "Do Not Sell My Personal Information" so people can opt-out of that practice. Selling the personal information of children below the age of 16-years-old has even more stringent requirements. Such as a default opt-in process for consent and a button and other permission requests that would surely raise privacy and security concerns for would-be customers. Your company can avoid the need for such a button by not selling customer information.

As the consumer privacy act was written and passed very quickly, and many questions have already been brought up about various loopholes and how certain provisions will be enforced. Nonetheless the focus is on consumer privacy and the determination that companies which trade in personal information are rigorously regulated. You can expect that the State of California will issue revisions and amendments before the consumer privacy act goes into effect in 2020 but the overarching principles of the Act are unlikely to change significantly.

A common belief is that the CCPA will be usurped shortly by a national federal privacy regulation so why bother? Indeed, many of the tech companies through the Internet Association are lobbying for a federal law. Indeed the Internet Association, which has as members Google, Facebook and Amazon, are lobbying hard and trying to position themselves as key contributors and influencers on the drafting of any consumer privacy bill. However, so long as the Republican Party controls the presidency and both houses of Congress, the probability of there being significant change to the national privacy and anti-spam laws is nil. However, if the balance of power is different after the elections in 2020, the CCPA could be a catalyst for national changes.

In any case with the CCPA coming into force in 2020 companies that do fall under its jurisdiction will have no option but to comply with the new law. However, in such an unstable climate where significant changes may occur to the articles and recitals and hence the compliance requirements before 2020 how can businesses prepare for compliancy with the CCPA?

Issues and Damages for Non-Compliance

When contemplating compliance with any new regulation the board and the executives of a company tend to think along well defines lines. Firstly, what is the cost of non-compliance? Secondly, what is the cost of compliancy? Thirdly, how can we mitigate the risk of con-compliance?

To address the first question on the CEO's lips, "What is the cost of non-compliance?" Well with reference to the EU GDPR the answer got the board's attention and immediate prioritisation — 4% of annual global turnover or €20 Million (whichever is greater). The CCPA is not nearly as punitive, but the penalties are not exactly light but they do have the potential in the case of a major breach to mount up to extremely large amounts. This is because unlike under most privacy laws in the U.S., there is a new private cause of action (which can include class-actions). Damages range from between $100 and $750 per consumer per incident for statutory or actual damages, whichever is greater, injunctive or declaratory relief, or "any other relief the court deems proper".

There are limitations, which are designed to give businesses an opportunity to minimise their liability including that before a claim is filed for statutory damages, a business must be given 30 days prior notice and if a cure is possible and it is actually cured, no claim may proceed. This notice requirement does not apply for a claim of actual damages. There is also a requirement that a consumer bringing an action must notify the Attorney General within 30 days that the action has been filed. If the AG decides to prosecute the action for the violation, then the private right of action cannot move forward.

The damages for actions brought by the AG include a civil penalty per violation provided under Section 17206 of the Business and Professions Code (generally up to $2,500 per violation), and up to $7,500 for each intentional violation under Section 1798.155(b) of the CCPA.

Note that the private right of action is limited in scope and does not apply to general violations of the CCPA. Thus, a cause of private right of action therefore requires establishing all three of the prerequisites: (1) the data is unencrypted or non-redacted; (2) is subject to an unauthorized access and exfiltration, theft, or disclosure; and (3) a generalized requirement that the "data breach" was a result of a failure to implement reasonable security procedures and practices.

Therefore, exercising a private right of action would require considerable legal and technical guidance, for instance the expert level knowledge of IT, privacy and security experts will be necessary in order to prove up each of these elements.

In addition, note that a claim for statutory damages cannot move forward if a business has "cured" its violation. How a business is expected to cure a data breach is not expanded upon but the consensus of security practitioners is that once a "breach" has happened, it is not possible to provide a cure, other than to take measures to prevent it from happening again. An alternative motive is perhaps it provides a 30 day grace period for a business to prove that no loss or damage occurred due to sufficient controls being in place – encryption or redaction. This may be included in order to attempt to limit the number of gratuitous actions taken by consumers who have not suffered actual harm.

The following are some additional nuances regarding the CCPA that a business planning for CCPA compliance should contemplate:

Application to Residents of California: The CCPA applies to a natural person who is a resident of California. It does not apply to, for example, the collection or sale of data "wholly" outside of the State of California, which means "if the business collected that information while the consumer was outside of California, no part of the sale of the consumer's personal information occurred in California, and no personal information collected while the consumer was in California is sold." AB 375 § 1798.145(a)(6).

Application to Certain Businesses: The CCPA applies to a business that: (1) has greater than $25,000,000 in revenue; (2) sells or shares for commercially purposes the personal information of 50,000 or more consumers, households, or devices; OR (3) derives 50 percent or more of its annual revenues from selling consumers' personal information.

Right of Deletion: Subject to exceptions, there is a general right for a consumer to request deletion of any personal information collected by the business (and this would extend to any third-party suppliers of the business). However, data must be found in order to be deleted, which is typically the major stumbling block.

Expanded Definition of Personal Information: There is an expanded definition of "personal information," which includes additions such as "geolocation", "inferences", "tendencies", but these are new criteria not uniformly included in other similar laws.

Right to Opt-Out (for sale of personal information): Not surprisingly, a business may only sell a consumer's personal information if the consumer is given a right to opt-out. A business and its service providers must stop selling a consumer's personal information once a consumer has opted-out. The CCPA places the burden on the consumer to opt-out of the organization's data collection practices, as compared to the GDPR which requires the consumer to take affirmative action to opt-in before continuing to the website. Under the CCPA, a business must do the following (among other things):

- Without requiring a consumer to create an account, provide a clear and conspicuous link on the business' Internet homepage, titled "Do Not Sell My Personal Information," to an Internet Web page that enables a consumer to opt out of the sale of the consumer's personal information.
- Include a description of a consumer's rights, along with a separate link to the "Do Not Sell My Personal Information" Internet Web page in its online privacy policy or policies if the business has an online privacy policy or policies, and

any California-specific description of consumers' privacy rights.

Notice and Methods for Submitting Requests for Disclosure: If you collect consumers' personal information you must, at or before the point of collection, inform consumers as to the categories of personal information to be collected and the purposes for which the categories of personal information shall be used. A business must also provide consumers at least two methods for submitting requests for information required to be disclosed including, at a minimum, a toll-free telephone number, and if the business maintains an Internet Website, a Website address.

Disclosure Obligations: Unlike the GDPR, the consumer must take affirmative steps to enjoy the rights and protections afforded to it under the CCPA. Upon receipt of a "verifiable request" by a consumer, a business is required within 45 days to provide the consumer with the categories and specific pieces of personal information the business has collected (with some exceptions and limitations, such as no more than 2x in a 12-month period and a possible extension of the 45 days). Depending on the type of business, this may include the following:

- The categories of personal information it has collected about that consumer.
- The categories of sources from which the personal information is collected.
- The business or commercial purpose for collecting or selling personal information.
- The categories of third parties with whom the business shares personal information.

- The specific pieces of personal information it has collected about that consumer.
- The categories of personal information that the business sold about the consumer, and the categories of third parties to whom the personal information was sold, by category or categories of personal information for each third party to whom the personal information was sold.
- Disclosure by the business that it has not disclosed the consumer's personal information for a business purpose.

Training: Adequate training is required for individuals responsible for handling all consumer inquiries about a business's privacy practice, compliance with the CCPA, and how to direct consumers to exercise their rights under the CCPA.

Updating Privacy Policies and Notices: There are other provisions requiring disclosure in privacy policies: the information above (and update every 12 months), a description of most of the rights of consumers under the CCPA, a list of the categories of information it has collected, and a list of categories of personal information it has sold or disclosed for a business purpose. Most companies already have special notices already embedded in their privacy policies as required, and it seems like this may be a good time to amend and revise policies as a whole.

Third Parties: Ensure you have third party agreements in writing before you share personal information with any third parties. A business must ensure that third parties comply with CCPA (although it is notable that the CCPA does not make a business liable for its third parties that it shares or sells personal information to if it has a written contract with them and, at the time of disclosure, it did not have actual knowledge or reason to believe that the third party intends to violate the restriction).

Minors: There are special restrictions and obligations with respect to minors.

Summary of compliance requirements

The CCPA's requirements can be grouped into three technical domains –those that relate to individual rights, those that relate to data security, and those that relate to service providers. The following provides a cross reference between the core requirements of the CCPA and the functional policies and procedures that organizations should consider putting into place as part of their compliance strategy.

The CCPA confers data privacy protection for Californian residents and as such provides certain rights under the law. These individual rights are:

- ☑ Privacy Notices to data subjects (The right to know what personal information is collected and whether it is disclosed);
- ☑ Right to request access to personal information;
- ☑ Right to request deletion of personal information collected from the consumer (aka The Right to be Forgotten);
- ☑ Right to opt out of the sale of the consumer's personal information; and
- ☑ Right to opt-in to the sale of consumer personal information for minors
- ☑ Right to receive services on equal terms
- ☑ Right to receive collected personal information that a business has free of charge by mail or in a readily usable

electronic format that allows the consumer to transmit the information to another entity.

In order to be compliant with the CCPA requires a diligent approach to data governance, security and privacy. A huge bonus when contemplating compliance for CCPA or any consumer privacy regulation for that matter is when the company has an existing culture that is respectful of the privacy of their consumers. The concept of Transparency is one of the fundamental pillars that underpin the CCPA framework. The privacy act already places extensive and in some cases specific obligations on organisations to be fair, open and honest about the ways that they use information about Californian residents and individual's personal data. Crucially, the concept of transparency relates to the requirement that organisations be fair, open and truthful with consumers as to the what, why, who, where and how in relation to the processing of their private data. Adhering to this principle alone is a major step toward compliancy.

Privacy notices

A privacy notice (sometimes referred to as a privacy policy or an information notice) is a document provided by a company to data subjects that includes, among other things, a description of what types of personal data the company collects, how the company uses that data, with whom the company shares the data, and how the company protects the data.

The CCPA requires that a business provide those Californians about whom it has collected personal information, information about the organization's privacy practices. The privacy notice should typically be given "at or before the point of collection" of the information.

Compliance To-Do List

- ☑ Review existing privacy notices and verify that they meet each of the new requirements of the CCPA.
- ☑ Identify instances in which you may be collecting information about Californians and do not currently have a privacy notice.
- ☑ In such situations, draft a privacy notice that conforms with both the CCPA and with other privacy laws that may apply (e.g., the GDPR).

Right to access data

The right to access data refers to the ability of a person to request that a business confirm whether it has personal information about him or her, the type of personal information that the business keeps about the individual, and/or a copy of the specific information that the business has on file. Access requests are sometimes referred to as Data Subject Access Requests, DSARs, or SARs.

Compliance To-Do List

- ☑ Review existing methods for submitting access requests to your organization to verify that they comply with the CCPA.
- ☑ Review existing policies or procedures for authenticating individuals that make access requests.

- ☑ If no authentication policy exists, draft an appropriate policy for authentication of individuals that make data subject requests.
- ☑ Draft a "play book" that provides standard communications that can be sent to individuals that make access requests, and standard formats for reporting personal information.
- ☑ Train employees on the handling of access requests.
- ☑ Verify that the policy in-place facilitates the fulfillment of access requests within the time period permitted by the statute.

Right to be forgotten

The right to be forgotten (sometimes called the right of erasure or the right to deletion) refers to the ability of a person to request that a business delete the personal information that it holds about them. The right to be forgotten is often misinterpreted as being an absolute right when, in reality, it only applies in a limited number of situations.

Compliance To-Do List

- ☑ Review existing methods for submitting deletion requests to your organization to verify that they comply with the CCPA.
- ☑ Review existing policies or procedures for authenticating individuals that make deletion requests.
- ☑ If no authentication policy exists, draft an appropriate policy for authentication of individuals that make data subject requests

- ☑ Draft a "play book" that provides standard communications that can be sent to individuals that make deletion requests.
- ☑ Train employees on the handling of deletion requests.
- ☑ Verify that the policy in-place facilitates the fulfillment of deletion requests within the time period permitted by the statute.
- ☑ Review protocols for deleting personal information.
- ☑ Review technological capability for doing a "hard delete" (i.e., an irrevocable deletion) and a "selective deletion" (i.e., deleting one individual's information without corrupting a larger information system) from live systems.

Right to opt-out from having information sold

The right to opt-out refers to the ability of a person to direct that a business cannot sell the personal information that it holds about them.

Compliance To-Do List

- ☑ Review existing privacy notices and verify that they meet the new requirements of the CCPA.
- ☑ Ensure websites include a "Do Not Sell My Personal Information" link.
- ☑ If no methods exist, establish appropriate methods for submitting opt-out requests to your organization that comply with the CCPA.
- ☑ Draft an appropriate policy for the authentication of individuals that make opt-out requests.
- ☑ Draft a "play book" that provides standard communications that can be sent to individuals that make opt-out requests.

☑ Train employees on how to handle opt-out requests.

☑ Verify that the policies in place facilitate the fulfillment of opt-out requests for the period of time required by the CCPA.

Right to opt-in to having information sold (minors)

The right to opt-in refers to the requirement within the CCPA that a business cannot sell the personal information of a consumer that is less than 16 years old unless the business has received "opt-in" consent – i.e. the affirmative authorization for the sale of the information. If a child is between the ages of 13 and 16 they can provide the necessary opt-in consent directly to the business. If a child is under the age of 13, a parent or guardian must provide the consent.

Compliance To-Do List

☑ Identify whether your business is knowingly collecting information from children under the age of 16.

☑ Identify whether your business may be unknowingly collecting information from children under the age of 16.

☑ Institute a system for collecting parental consent prior to the collection of information from children.

☑ Verify that the consent mechanism complies with the CCPA, COPPA, and/or the GDPR.

☑ Train employees on how to handle inquiries relating to the information collected about a child.

Right to receive services on equal terms

The "right to equal service and price" refers to the CCPA's prohibition against discriminating against consumers who exercise their rights under the CCPA. Where a consumer exercises a right, a business is prohibited from denying goods or services, charging a different price, imposing penalties, providing a different level or quality of service, or suggesting the consumer will receive a different price or rate or different level or quality of goods or services.

Compliance To-Do List

- ☑ Review your business's pricing policies and practices to verify that they do not price discriminate – intentionally or inadvertently – based upon whether a person opts-out of the sale of their information.
- ☑ Review existing privacy notices and verify that they meet the new requirements of the CCPA.
- ☑ Draft an appropriate policy for managing requests by consumers who exercise their rights under the CCPA.
- ☑ Train employees on how to handle and document requests by consumers who exercise their rights under the CCPA.
- ☑ Verify that policies in place facilitate compliance with the new requirements of the CCPA for consumers who exercise their rights.

▍Data security

"A business . . . shall implement and maintain reasonable security procedures and practices appropriate to the nature of the information, to protect the personal information from unauthorized access, destruction, use, modification, or disclosure."

The CCPA requires that organizations put into place "reasonable security procedures and practices" to help protect personal information from being breached. If information is breached and the breach happens "as a result of" an organization's failure to implement reasonable security, the statute permits impacted individuals to bring suit to recover a statutory liquidated damage of between $100 and $750 per consumer per incident.

Compliance To-Do List

- ☑ Memorialize security policies and procedures in a written information security plan or "WISP."
- ☑ Review whether your WISP conforms to a known industry standard or framework.
- ☑ Consider whether there are any security policies or procedures that have not been drafted, but should be included within your WISP.
- ☑ Review the substance of your WISP on an annual basis.
- ☑ Conduct periodic risk assessments to identify the primary risks to information.
- ☑ Train employees on your security policies and procedures.

Service Provider Agreements

The CCPA allows businesses to share personal information with third parties or service providers for business purposes so long as there is a written contract that complies with the CCPA. Among other things, the CCPA prohibits any agreement or contract provision that seeks to waive or limit a consumer's rights under the CCPA.

Compliance To-Do List

- ☑ Review existing agreements with service providers to identify potential gaps.
- ☑ Identify instances in which you may be using a service provider that has access to information about Californians and with whom you do not currently have agreements in place.
- ☑ Update agreements with service providers to ensure that they meet the new requirements of the CCPA.

Frequently Asked Questions

FAQ 1: Who receives new rights under CCPA? What is a "consumer"?

Under CCPA, a consumer is a California "resident" as defined in California's personal income tax regulations, i.e., any natural person "enjoying the benefit and protection of [California] laws and government" who is in California "for other than a temporary or transitory purpose" or "domiciled" in California but "outside the State for a temporary or transitory purpose." This though is being hotly disputed by the lobbyists for the business coalition who want to see a much more narrow and precise definition so this will be one of the strategic targets in the battle ahead in 2019.

FAQ 2: What is the definition of "personal information" to which CCPA applies?

CCPA defines "personal information" as information that "identifies, relates to, describes, is capable of being associated with, or could reasonably be linked, directly or indirectly, with a particular consumer or household."

This definition is broader than the Federal Trade Commission's definition of personal information and similar in scope to the definition of personal data under GDPR.

To illustrate, but not limit, its broad definition of personal information, CCPA enumerates eleven specific categories:

(i)   identifiers, such as a "unique personal identifier" (a defined term) and "online identifier Internet Protocol address";

(ii)   "characteristics of protected classifications under California or federal law";

(iii)   "commercial information," such as including records of products or services purchased and other purchasing or consuming histories or tendencies;

(iv)   biometric information, a defined term that means physiological, biological and behavioural characteristics and includes the traditional fingerprint and retinal scan but also keystroke and gait patterns as well as "sleep, health and exercise data that contain identifying information";

(v)   "Internet or other electronic network activity information," such as browsing history or "interaction ... with an advertisement";

(vi)   geolocation data;

(vii)   audio, electronic, visual, thermal, olfactory or similar information;

(viii) professional or employment-related information;

(ix)   education information that is not public as defined in the federal Family Educational Rights and Privacy Act[19], and

(x)   inferences, which is a defined term meaning the "derivation of information ... assumptions, or conclusions from ... another source of information," derived from data drawn from any of the information identified above to create a profile about a consumer's "preferences, characteristics, psychological trends, preferences [sic], predispositions, behaviour, attitudes, intelligence, abilities, and aptitudes."

Again the definition for personal information in the context of the Act is far too broad for the liking of the business coalition. This will be something they lobby hard for in 2019.

FAQ 3: What information is excluded from CCPA's definition of personal information?

CCPA's definition of personal information excludes "publicly available information," which means information "lawfully made available from federal, state, or local government records, if any conditions associated with such information" but excludes biometric information collected without the consumer's knowledge and personal information used for a purpose different from the one for which the data is maintained and made available in the government records or otherwise publicly maintained.

Personal information also does not include "de-identified" consumer information, which cannot "reasonably identify ... or be linked to" a particular person, or "aggregate" consumer information, which is "not linked or reasonably linkable to any consumer or household, including via a device". Also excepted from CCPA is personal information:

- collected, used, sold or disclosed pursuant to the Gramm-Leach-Blilely Act or the Driver's Privacy Protection Act of 1995, but only if CCPA "is in conflict" with those laws; and
- sold to or from a consumer reporting agency (as defined in the Fair Credit Reporting Act) when the personal information is "reported in, or used to generate," a consumer credit report.

FAQ 4: What is the definition for Publicly Available information?

Under the CCPA, Personal Information is not information that is "publicly available." The statute provides greater insight into this definition: Publicly available, means information that is lawfully made available from federal, state, or local government records, if any conditions associated with such Information [sic]. Hence publicly available does not mean biometric information collected by a business about a consumer without the consumer's knowledge. Information is not publicly available if that data is used for a purpose that is not compatible with the purpose for which the data is maintained and made available in the government records or for which it is publicly maintained. "Publicly available" does not include consumer information that is deidentified or aggregate consumer information.

It is all too easy to glance over that and miss the significant change in a relatively benign everyday business phrase. Nonetheless, there is a lot of significant change to this definition, including the fact that "publicly available" does not include the classic definition i.e., information that is already made public by private parties. There is also the concept that in order to be publicly available, it must be used for a purpose that is compatible with which it was first maintained—meaning that it is not just how data is gathered, but also the way it is used must now be consistent with the purpose of its first collection. This concept of usage that remains consistent with the data's first collection is one that can present significant challenges. Many businesses harvest public available data from sources that are providing information to the public for a purpose that is certainly not compatible with the company's business models.

FAQ 5: What businesses must comply with CCPA? Does CCPA apply to non-profits?

CCPA applies to a for-profit entity that:

- collects consumers' personal information directly or through a third party; and
- alone or jointly determines the purposes and means of the processing of consumers' personal information; and does business in the State of California; and meets one of the following thresholds: has annual gross revenues in excess of $25,000,000;

- alone or in combination, annually buys, receives for the business' commercial purposes, sells, or shares for commercial purposes, alone or in combination, the personal information of 50,000 or more consumers, households, or devices; and
- derives 50 percent or more of its annual revenues from selling consumers' personal information.

California is the world's fifth largest economy, and as a result CCPA covers a large number of businesses inside and outside California. It is unclear at this point whether the $25,000,000 threshold encompasses worldwide or only California annual gross revenue. And, as drafted, the economic thresholds will sweep in many small businesses that do not meet the $25,000,000 gross revenue threshold. Any entity that controls or is controlled by a business and shares common branding with a business that meets the above criteria also is subject to CCPA.

A non-profit entity is not subject to CCPA because it does not operate "for the profit or financial benefit" of its owners.

A "covered entity" subject to the Health Insurance Portability and Accountability Act of 1996[33] is not subject to CCPA with respect to the protected health information ("PHI") that it collects from a consumer but could be subject to CCPA for any personal information (as defined in CCPA) collected that is not PHI.

FAQ 6: How is a Sale of Personal Information Different from a Disclosure for a "Business Purpose"?

CCPA defines "sell" broadly to include any communication or transfer of consumer's personal information by a CCPA-covered business to a third party "for monetary or other valuable consideration." Disclosing personal information for a "business purpose" is different because the disclosure is for one of the enumerated "operational" purposes of the CCPA-covered business or its service provider.

A business generally may sell personal information orally, in writing, electronically or by "other means." CCPA excludes the following from its definition of a sale:

- when a consumer uses or directs — through "one or more deliberate interactions" — the business to intentionally disclose personal information to a third party, as long as the third party does not subsequently sell the personal information (unless the sale is otherwise permitted under CCPA);
- when a business uses or shares an identifier to inform others that the consumer has exercised the right to opt out;
- when a business uses or shares personal information with a service provider "necessary to perform a business purposes [sic]", if: the business already provided CCPA-compliant notice about the use or sharing; and
- the service provider does not use the transferred personal information except as necessary to perform the business purpose; or
- when a transfer of personal information that is part of a merger, acquisition, bankruptcy, or other transaction in which a third party assumes control of the business (in whole or part), if the transferee continues to honour the

right to know and right to access, including notifying consumers in advance if the transferee will use or share the personal information in a new or different way.

"Business purposes" are:

"auditing" the interaction with the consumer and concurrent transactions, including counting ad impressions, verifying quality of ad impressions and "auditing compliance with this specification and other standards";

- detecting or preventing security incidents;
- debugging;
- short-term, transient use if the personal information is not disclosed and not used to build a profile or "otherwise alter an individual consumer's experience outside the current interaction," such as for "contextual customization of ads shown as part of the same interaction" (i.e., interest-based advertising);
- performing services on behalf of a CCPA-covered business or its service provider, such as customer service, order fulfillment, payment processing, financing and advertising, marketing or analytic services;
- undertaking internal research for "technological development and demonstration"; and
- verifying or maintaining quality or safety or improving or upgrading a service or device owned, manufactured or controlled by or for the business.

Any use of personal information for a business purpose must be reasonably necessary for, and proportionate to, the purpose for which the personal information is first processed or another contextually "compatible" operational purpose.

FAQ 7: What Is a "Verifiable Consumer Request" and How Does a Business Respond to One?

CCPA defines a "verifiable consumer request" ("VCR") as a request made by or on behalf of a consumer to exercise his or her CCPA rights for which a business can reasonably verify the identity of the consumer or the consumer's representative.

For the right to know and right to opt out, a CCPA-covered business must offer at least two methods for VCR submission. One of these two methods must be a toll-free number and the other a website address (if the business has a website). A business is required to respond to only two (2) requests from the same consumer over a 12-month period. The VCR process must be free of charge to the consumer.

For any VCR, the business must respond in writing either through the consumer's account with the business if the consumer maintains an account with the business or, if the consumer does not maintain an account with the business, the consumer's choice of mail or electronic communication. Once a consumer has submitted the VCR, the business has 45 days to respond and, as long as the business notifies the consumer within the first 45 days that additional time is needed, up to 45 more days (or a total of 90 days). The response to the VCR must cover the 12-month period preceding the date on which the business received the VCR.

By June 28, 2019, the California Attorney General is required to adopt regulations to help businesses determine when a request is a VCR. CCPA deems a consumer's request "submitted through a password-protected account maintained by the consumer with the business while the consumer is logged into the account" as a VCR. But, a business may not require a consumer to create an account in order to submit a VCR.

FAQ 8: How Does CCPA Apply To A Service Provider That Processes Personal Information For A CCPA-Covered Business?

A "service provider" is a for-profit entity that processes information on behalf of a CCPA-covered business. CCPA requires that the business (i) enter into a written contract with the service provider prohibiting the service provider from undertaking any processing of the personal information other than for the specific purpose of performing the services specified in the written contract and (ii) obtain "certification" that the service provider understands these restrictions. When requested, the service provider must delete personal information it processes for the CCPA-covered business, subject to the same exceptions to the right to delete as the covered business.

The service provider is liable for its own violations of CCPA, and the business that discloses the personal information to the service provider also will be liable for the service provider's CCPA violations if the business had "actual knowledge or reason to believe" that the service provider intended to violate CCPA.

FAQ 9: Does CCPA Have Exceptions?

CCPA does not apply to a business that processes personal information when the personal information is used to:

- comply with federal, state, or local laws or a civil, criminal, or regulatory inquiry, investigation, subpoena, or summons;
- cooperate with law enforcement agencies;
- exercise or defend legal claims;
- process "de-identified" information or "aggregate consumer information"; or
- collect or sell personal information when "every aspect of that commercial conduct takes place wholly outside of California" — that is, CCPA does not apply if all personal information was collected while the person to whom the personal information relates was outside of California and no part of the sale of the personal information occurred in California.

CCPA also does not apply if compliance would violate evidentiary privileges given under California law.

FAQ 10: What Are The Penalties For Violating CCPA? Does CCPA Have a Private Right Of Action?

The California Attorney General enforces CCPA, except that CCPA offers only a private right of action for "unauthorized access and exfiltration, theft, or disclosure" (i.e., a data breach).

Attorney General Action

Prior to initiating an action for a CCPA violation, the California Attorney General must give the offending business, service provider or other person not less than 30 days to cure the alleged violation. Thereafter:

- a business, service provider, or other person that negligently violates CCPA is subject to a civil penalty not to exceed $2,500 for each violation; and
- a business, service provider or other person that intentionally violates CCPA is liable for a civil penalty of up to $7,500 per violation.

Private Right of Action

A business may face a privacy right of action if it fails to implement and maintain reasonable security procedures and practices appropriate to the sensitivity of personal information processed by the business that causes a data breach. Specifically, the consumer may recover the greater of statutory damages of $100 to $750 "per consumer per incident" and actual damages. In determining statutory damages, a court must evaluate the nature, seriousness and persistence of the violations, the number of violations, the length of times over which the violations occurred, the willfulness of the violations, and the business' "assets, liabilities and net worth."

Before filing a lawsuit against the business for unreasonable security procedures, however, the consumer must provide 30 days' advance notice to the business of the allegedly violations:

If the business cures the alleged violation and provides the consumer "an express written statement that the violations have been cured and that no further violations shall occur," the consumer cannot proceed with the lawsuit.

If the business continues with its alleged violations, the consumer can file a lawsuit for the original, and any new, CCPA violation, including breaching the written statement.

No notice is required if the consumer suffered actual pecuniary damages as a result of the business' failure to implement and maintain reasonable security procedures.

The consumer also must notify the California Attorney General within 30 days after filing the lawsuit. The Attorney General then has 30 days to decide whether to prosecute the violation, to allow the consumer to proceed with his or her private action, or to notify the consumer that "the consumer shall not proceed with the action."

FAQ 10 - The Business is GDPR Compliant will we be CCPA Compliant?

What's important for companies to understand is that GDPR compliance does not equal CCPA compliance. To avoid major financial penalties, enterprises must take this on-board and get ready to address both sets of rules separately, ensuring that they have done their due diligence when it comes to protecting consumer data.

Both statutes, GDPR and CCPA, have the same starting point: the premise that data privacy is a fundamental right. Beyond that premise, there are a few other specific areas in CCPA that are recognizable to those familiar with GDPR, which include the "right to be forgotten," the "right to portability," and the "right to access data." Nonetheless, the similarities that the new California act has with GDPR or influence that the latter had in crafting the former, CCPA requires different compliance thresholds.

One major difference is how these rights are delivered in so much as GDPR defines privacy by default and design. This model requires consumers (data subjects) to opt-in by taking affirmative action to provide their consent – silence or inaction is not consent. The CCPA on the other hand takes the opt-out path where consumers must take affirmative action to exercise their rights of privacy as by default they are giving their consent.

Another major discrepancy between GDPR and CCPA is that the consumer has more rights to the preemption of the sale of the third party data before it happens - and to know the purpose of why their data is being collected and sold - via the CCPA than those in the EU. Specifically, CCPA will require that companies inform California residents what data the organization is collecting and how that information is being used. It also gives state residents the option to ask the company to delete the data or stop selling it. CCPA does not, however, prevent organizations from collecting people's data or give consumers the option to request that a company stop collecting their personal data, which differentiates the language from GDPR. There are many other differences but these are the most significant when addressing consumer rights and how they are delivered.

Lessons Learned from GDPR

GDPR can act as a good barometer as to how the California Consumer Privacy Act will perform in the real world post coming into operation. Although the GDPR has only been in effect since

25th May 2018 we can still learn a lot from its first 100 days. Interestingly, despite all the hype over the penalties, we have not seen any fines yet but that is down to regulators still investigating pre-GDPR violations and as it was made clear from the outset fines will be a last resort. Also the majority of businesses do appear to have taken compliance with the GDPR seriously. This is demonstrated through privacy notices appearing to be more transparent and consent forms more robust. But just because there has been no fines to date doesn't mean that the regulators are not undertaking detailed investigations albeit with limited resources so businesses should not become complacent.

There are a lot of regulatory investigations on-going so there will be fines. All the warning signs are there for those who know where to look. The most obvious performance metric to check is that people are exercising their rights more than before. However this increase in complaints has left regulators with capacity issues. For dealing with this surge in requests in a timely manner can be time and resource intensive. Hence, we can expect regulators to look unfavourably on any business consistently failing to meet their obligations.

Another major issue that legislators working on the CCPA need to be aware of is that the GDPR regulators have been flooded with breach notifications. Indeed, such has been the deluge of reported breaches it in itself is become a major issue for regulators to manage. The numbers are so high in fact that we have heard some noises from various regulators that businesses are notifying too much. But this is the unintentional consequence of a regime that threatens to severely punish a business for a failure to notify regulators of a breach and one where over-notification suffers no penalty. Hence it is little wonder that businesses are playing safe and reporting every breach no matter how trivial.

Nonetheless, the number of complaints for the public has also increased, and regulators are already dealing with huge backlogs. Therefore, businesses should prepare for the possibility that some of the complaints already filed could be about them.

Furthermore, businesses in just the first 3 months are beginning to see that in the rush to get 'something in place', they were not properly road-testing the "GDPR solutions" that they implemented. Indeed some of the solutions have been just too complicated or onerous for businesses to maintain day-to-day. Examples include the complicated Article 30 record that now needs to be kept up-to-date, or the 25-step 'online DPIA solution'. Businesses are quickly realising that maintaining these compliance solutions is time-wasting and an onerous task that is taking a toll on operational efficiency.

With over 100 days now passed, businesses are beginning to take a critical look at the controls and measures that they put in place before the GDPR deadline to see if they are fit for purpose. Some practical ways to do this might include:

- Conducting practical testing.
- Asking for honest feedback from the team members with day-to-day responsibility.
- If issues are identified, businesses shouldn't be afraid to change their approach.

After all if the controls and measures are troublesome to manage and operate eventually people will find ways to circumvent them.

Solutions like these are not only ineffective compliance measures they become compliance risks.

Some of the options might be:

- Considering whether the same level of compliance could be achieved by cutting away the complexity and keeping it simple.
- Identifying areas where technology can assist. There are lots of great software solutions out there so be sure to get one that addresses a specific business need.

We can learn a lot from the lessons learned by businesses undertaking similar regulatory compliance initiatives when undertaking a CCPA compliance project. Some of the profound lessons learned so far from the GDPR:

- Keep compliance controls and procedures as simple as possible. Considering whether the same level of compliance could be achieved by cutting away the complexity.
- Automate where possible and Identify areas where technology can assist.
- Don't just deploy compliance software for the sake of it there are a myriad of software solutions out there so be sure to get one that addresses a specific business need.
- Be prepared for a surge in requests from the public now that they are empowered and eager to exercise their new rights.

Consolidate and Secure Personal Information

Even if the business is compliant for GDPR, any business collecting or in possession of California resident data can't grow complacent.

Indeed the CCPA raises the bar for an even higher level of data security. Hence, companies should plan to first focus on data consolidation and then security in light of this new environment. How a business goes about deploying compliancy controls and procedures is dependent on the information ecosystem. Enterprises over the last few years have started to diverge in the way they manage information. Some are disciples of a centralised strategy where it's more efficient and easier to secure a single repository—plus perform search, review, production, and retention/disposition on the data—instead of trying to work with multiple application repositories with varying capabilities and rules. Others however have gone down the decentralised road where microservice architectures are creating hundreds if not thousands of diverse data bases spread across the entire network. Businesses pick the strategy that performs well for their core business and as such the compliancy methodology must match that design. Either way consolidating and securing personal information is a primary goal of any compliancy initiative.

The new California state law also will force companies to increase their awareness of exactly what consumer data they are collecting, why they are collecting it and if it is necessary how to find a way to manage that data more granularly. Despite the fact that the CCPA doesn't become operational to 2020 it's again time to ramp up and get prepared for the new California privacy law. What's more, don't be surprised if this pattern repeats itself when other states follow suit and adopt their own consumer data privacy legislation. While it's possible that other states will decide to adopt California's law, we also could end up with a patchwork of requirements if each state designs their own customized privacy regulation. That of course would be a disaster as one of the motivators for introducing the GDPR was to harmonise the privacy laws across all 29 EU states. To avoid that patchwork of legislation perhaps will require federal regulation. That scenario is favoured by some but for now the California Consumer Privacy Act is signed into law and that is what we will have to work with.

30975795R00134

Made in the USA
San Bernardino, CA
01 April 2019